Some Buyers Will, Some Buyers Won't.

With 27 years fashion experience, I explain how professionals target, attract & secure orders from international women's & men's fashion & accessory buyers, responsible for the world's premier and most sought after independent, department store and online retailers.

© 2012 Lulu Author. All rights reserved.
ISBN 978-1-4710-6049-6

All contents copyright ©2012 by Renato Grant. All rights reserved. No part of this document or the related files may be reproduced or transmitted in any form, by any means (electronic, photocopying, recording, or otherwise) without the prior written permission of the author or publisher.

Limit of Liability and Disclaimer of Warranty: The publisher has used its best efforts in preparing this book, and the information provided herein is provided "as is." Renato Grant makes no representation or warranties with respect to the accuracy or completeness of the contents of this book and specifically disclaims any implied warranties of merchantability or fitness for any particular purpose and shall in no event be liable for any loss of profit or any other commercial damage, including but not limited to special, incidental, consequential, or other damages.

Trademarks: This book identifies product names and services known to be trademarks, registered trademarks, or service marks of their respective holders. They are used throughout this book in an editorial fashion only. In addition, terms suspected of being trademarks, registered trademarks, or service marks have been appropriately capitalized, although Renato Grant cannot attest to the accuracy of this information. Use of a term in this book should not be regarded as affecting the validity of any trademark, registered trademark, or service mark. Renato Grant is not associated with any product or supplier mentioned in this book.

This book is dedicated to a number of people who have been, and still are, instrumental in my life.

Gifi Fields & Jeffrey Rogers for seeing in a younger me, things I never saw in myself and for setting me off on my path.

My daughter India, for whom I live, love & die for.

Mary, for her unswerving support & dedication, love & madness which keeps me alert and alive.

My Sister's, Nieces and closest friends Brian & Rods, Nigel, Mevs and Alex for always being there.

Contents

Chapter 1- The Beginning……………………………………….Page 5 - 8

Chapter 2- Introduction ……………………………………............Page 9-10

Chapter 3- Attracting Orders……………………………………Page 11-17

Chapter 4 - How important is your paperwork?..............................Page 18-22

Chapter 5- The exhibition space, showroom space tradeoff!..........Page 23-25

Chapter 6 - Getting paid………………………………………...Page 26-28

Chapter 7- The fashion calendar…………………………………..Page 29-30

Chapter 8- Production/cmt prices & fabrication costs……………Page 31-36

Chapter 9- Design……………………………………………..Page 37-38

Chapter 10- The collection is complete…………………………Page 39-41

Chapter 11- Creating the hype……………………………………..Page 42-43

Chapter 12- To e or not to e?..Page 44-46

Chapter 13- Agents, Showrooms & distributors…………………...Page 47-51

Chapter 14 - Why some labels succeed where others fail…………Page 52-56.

Chapter 15- Conclusion……………………………………………..Page 57-59

Costing sheet example & explanation……………………Page 61-62

UK Terms & Conditions………………………………………….Page 63-64

Trade reference form……………………………………………..Page 65

Tips & Tricks……………………………………………………...Page 66-68

The Top 400 plus Men's & Women's buyer & retail directory……..Page 69-206

A list of the best London fashion sales agencies and showrooms…Page 207-209

Chapter 1

The Beginning

It's 1985 and as a 19 year old teenager living at home, I desperately needed a job, having scanned the daily newspapers I applied for a warehouse position within a fashion company in central London.

I was to be the last to be interviewed that day so I had good opportunity to check out the competition going up before me. Everyone looked trendy; I looked like a teenager from a London estate trying his best with what he had, as that was exactly what I was. I remember thinking to myself; no way would I ever get this position as I didn't have any experience or the 'look' to fit in, but would just relax and put it all down to a learning experience and go through it anyway.

After an hour's interview on a sofa within a large open planned room with everyone staring at me, I was offered the position! I thought I was being offered the position due to my relaxed and chilled interview technique, charm & skills, in later years I learned I was only offered the position because a young female employee, named Doreen Estro, who noticed me being interviewed liked my afro hairstyle! So much for my charm, style & presence.

That was with a London fashion house called Coppernob who are huge and still operate today. The owner, a crazy golden haired American ex-hippy type, Gifi Fields, was to become my mentor. I still bump into him occasionally at various buying offices and there is still no better fashion salesman than Gifi whom I admire greatly.

One day, whilst humping a dirty dusty 20kg roll of fabric on my shoulders through his plush showroom in the heart of London's West End, I noticed a guy sitting around a table, drinking wine talking to a very attractive young lady. I asked a colleague what he was doing, I was told he was presenting a fashion buyer this seasons collection, his job was showroom fashion sales. From that moment I decided that was Where I should & would be!

With exactly zero sales experience, I managed to blag my way into an interview for junior sales staff with another fashion house called Jeffrey Rogers. In that interview I was asked by the owner, Jeffrey, to hold up one of his many designs and sell it to him. I waffled on and on, talking complete rubbish, until he laughed and said 'enough!'

He looked me dead in the eye and told me what I already knew, that I knew nothing. I got the job! He decided that if I was young, foolish & cocksure enough to try to blag him, then once polished I would be a confident, young cocksure salesman in front of buyers.

He talked of fine tuning me into a knowledgeable fashion salesman once I had learnt the ropes and so he started me off selling cheap t-shirts & knitwear in their hundreds and thousands to independent boutiques & small department store groups.

I was also responsible for a team of sales agents and had to pack their sample collections into boxes to be shipped to them so they could obtain orders for us. Once they had sold merchandise on our behalf, I had to collate all the orders and pass the details onto the production team. This was one of the most boring parts on the job and I didn't know it at the time but I was receiving fantastic experience for what was to happen later in my career, I day dreamed often. I did this for many years and it was my introduction to the world of fashion agents. At that point I said to myself; let's see how high I can ride this fashion thing as I referred to it back in those days.

Many years later, having experienced periods in fashion warehouses, pattern rooms, design rooms, quality control departments, shipping departments, CMT factories and sales showrooms, I was wholesaling $3000 couture dresses, by Maria Grachvogel, to departments stores such as Harvey Nichols & Harrods which were being worn by Saudi Princesses. I was being taken to exhibit at London Fashion Week, New York Fashion Week and Paris Fashion Week by Sara Sturgeon, who is still my favorite designer, I had the wife of the then Prime Minister in my showroom trying on designs I presented and asking about my family. I thought I had arrived.

Little did I know that the world of fashion sales is far from a glamorous one? Sure we may travel around the globe from exhibition to exhibition and show to show, but it is a hard and often thankless task. Nobody is that interested in our graft & roadwork which has resulted in a designer being stocked in Selfridges London or Barneys NY. The fashion press is interested in the designer, not the salesman. The buyers are interested in sales made in store not the salesman or woman who presented the collection to them. We are merely the mouth pieces, however the perks can be great and often we have a lot of fun along the way.

I have worked in the UK fashion industry, in varying sales roles, for 27 years. I started when I was 19, I am now 46. I have worked in many showrooms presenting global men's & women's fashion designers & brands, including Alannah Hill, Ginger & Smart, Maria Grachvogel, Sara Sturgeon, Exte, Roberto Cavalli mainline, Just Cavalli Jeans, Dolce & Gabbana and Versace jeans Couture.

With the above mentioned designers and brands I have supplied literally hundreds of top end boutiques, department stores and e-tailers over the years, both in the UK and Ireland as well as premier stores, throughout Europe, the Far East and the US. I have exhibited at London; Paris, Las Vegas & NY fashion weeks and have sold consistently for 20 of my 27 years in the industry.

Prior to my sales experience I had to learn the ropes so to speak starting in the warehouse, production, sampling & design rooms through to CMT factories to see how everything came together. Today I continue my journey in the fashion world where no two days are ever the same. There really is no other industry like it.

Fashion buyers operate in a world of their own, all are forever busy, some are lovely, polite and genuine, and others are not. This is not a dog eat dog world, but can, and often is, one where claws are sometimes in and sometimes out!

Buyers can be very protective over designers and brands that they stock and understandably so. In a world which appears dominated by mainstream commercial fashion on the high street, away from the high street independent boutiques rule and fashion buyers within these stores have pretty high expectations.

I have learned to treat everyone in the same manner, whether they are buying for a single independent boutique or for a large chain of department stores.

Success lies both in the products and the presentation, orders are not guaranteed therefore it pays to remember that some buyers will and some buyers won't place orders with you for a myriad of reasons. The actual skill in taking orders lies in our art of persuasion and the strategies we employ to get the desired results.

Chapter 2

Introduction

Many of today's popular & iconic fashion brands have started out by selling their fashion & accessory merchandise on market stalls. They aspired to having their products sold through premier retailers and they went for it. Some succeeded where others failed. The difference was some had an overall understanding of the industry and business, complimented by an effective sales & marketing campaign, whereas others did not.

Regardless of whether you are an emerging designer, new to the fashion business, a graduate or student of fashion or perhaps thinking of launching your own label, this book will give you a practical insight into what to do and what not to do in order to successfully sell to fashion, lifestyle & accessory buyers worldwide.

Fashion sales is perhaps one of the most under represented & unspoken about area's within fashion, yet without sales everything else become's redundant. A beautiful collection will remain simply a beautiful collection of samples if no sales orders are secured. A catwalk or photo shoot, a PR or marketing campaign without retailers stocking the merchandise becomes meaningless.

I have included everything that I have learned on my journey with a view to helping you to sell your merchandise to the same quality boutiques and departments stores that I do. Everything in this book relates to fashion sales within a wholesale environment. It looks at what is required to take your fashion products from showroom to retail and how buyers are enticed to view one collection over another.

Buyers the world over tend to make similar decisions when deciding which fashion collections to stock in a given season. Their choice of collection will always differ greatly, depending upon personal preference, customer type and location, however when choosing which labels they plan to view for the season, they base their decisions on a number of factors.

Every season, fashion buyers receive an enormous amount of information pre season from every designer and brand seeking to get in front of them. Clearly their choices can be influenced by press coverage and marketing as well as discoveries they have made themselves. A lot of information received is discarded simply due to presentation or more importantly, the lack of, whilst information well sent and packaged can jump to the top of the pile.

If you are reading this book, which at the rear contains full details of over 400 of the best UK retailers and e-tailers in the industry, then you are serious about selling your label/brand into one of the most influential fashion markets in the world, the UK.

Regardless of whether the UK is an important market for you or not, the details within the book represent typical approaches we make as fashion salespeople no matter if the US or far East happens to be your key market , the process is similar, if not the same.

The 400 top independent boutique buyers and department store buyers listed at the rear of the book refer to my domestic market, the UK. I doubt very much you will find a similar list in your domestic market without it costing a small fortune. The best method however is to develop your own list, this takes lots of roadwork and lots of time. Hopefully my book will offer a shortcut.

So here it is. This is what we do, as professional sales men and women in the fashion business, to have our collections firstly viewed and ultimately ordered by the very best retailers and e-tailers in the fashion business, worldwide.

Chapter 3

Attracting orders

To secure your first stockist, you have to work hard and there are no shortcuts. If you're an overseas designer and you are attracted to selling within the UK market, you must try to work in conjunction with your Embassy or trade body here in the UK and show at as many relevant sponsored trade exhibitions as possible. Your Embassy or trade body will have greater access to more area's within the industry than you do at the moment and can also provide extremely useful information regarding possible finance grants that may be available to you to assist with overseas exhibitions.

When applying to showcase your collections at specific trade shows, ensure that you research the exhibition first as the overall cost of the stands differ greatly and you must ensure that the tradeshow you plan to exhibit at is relevant to your product ranges.

For example, a stand at Pure London or Stitch menswear, two of our UK premier trade shows in London, will differ in cost to that of a static stand at London Fashion Week.

Fashion buyers do take great pleasure when meeting the designer and will feel privileged when presented the collection by the designer. Sales people tend to take over when it comes to talking through and writing of the orders. Buyers do like the collection presented by designers but prefer the speed of salespeople writing the orders because then they can also say certain things aloud in honesty (maybe pricing/styling/colour ways not too their liking etc) that they would not dream of saying to the designer, so as the designer you must know when to take a backseat. It also allows the buyer(s) to relax in the knowledge that salespeople are thicker skinned than the designers themselves.

If exhibitions are difficult for whatever reasons, then you must either mail the buyer your fantastic images, look book, or better still, go see the buyer at their store if able.

When planning to 'drop in' on a boutique, always call and enquire first. Just say that you're in the area for an hour and would it be okay to show a few of your designs which will probably take half an hour. If the buyer likes what she/he sees then you could be there a lot longer but it will be at their discretion. If they do not like what they see or it's not for them, you'll be in and out in less than 15 minutes.

With regards to mailing the buyers information, do not send them information that is too bulky or longwinded. It will get thrown away, why? Because they are sent too much from too many designers.

Yours has to stand out. Design something that is small enough and light enough to be carried in a shoulder bag, concise and shows images of your best pieces with just enough explanation of the collection on it to excite a buyer. If you have press pieces about your collection you could include this in your mail out. Include your website details also.

This works well because it tells buyers just enough about the collection, shows the best imagery and gives a little background. If you design a well sized postcard, these also work well because when it is delivered it is not in an envelope and so the likely hood is that it will get seen and if buyers like what they see on the front they will read what is on the back.

Sometimes buyers will take this postcard when they are out on buying appointments because it is lightweight and small enough to fit in a handbag and acts as a reminder as to what you offer and where you are based.

When I send my mail outs I make sure that they arrive either on a Tuesday, Wednesday or Thursday morning. Why? Because it's midweek, stores are usually quieter and buyers have more time to browse their mail! Also Monday's are when department store buyers do figures so never a good time for mail or calls and Fridays get busier in the lead up to the weekend. When I am making my follow up phone calls I call late morning after 11 am but before 3pm the same for the same reasons!

No point calling a buyer late afternoon, either they would have left the store already or, be on other appointments or more than likely they have customers in the store and may not take your call.

Buyers do not mind if you are prepared to take a small capsule collection to them but you must make sure to tell them it is a small capsule collection. They will not be too happy if you turn up with a 150 piece collection. They need the space to sell goods in store. If you call and ask if it will be okay to pop in and show a few pieces next time you are around, the likelihood is that they will say fine. This is a very good way of taking initial orders. It will cost the buyer nothing other than a small amount of time but show great enthusiasm on your part. I have done this many times and still do it today if there is no other way. I prefer showroom sales because I will have the full attention of my buyers but if I really want a store to buy my collections and they cannot get to me for any reason then I will go to them with collection and order book in hand.

If budgets are tight, as they usually are for us all, there is also no reason why PR cannot be done in-house and you should approach fashion editors & journalists directly with the view to having either editorial or product placement within their publications.

Press typically wants great images sent to them initially and a well written press release. Simply buy the top magazines, Vogue, Grazie, Stella, Marie Claire etc, find the page that lists all fashion editors/ assistants and make contact. It is a very big money saver for you and you will be doing a similar job PR's will do initially but charge you a lot of money. The advantage of course of being represented by a good PR is that they already have established relationships with fashion editors and journalists.

Magazines do call off samples if they feel it may fit an article or shoot they have upcoming and you will have to make the samples readily available.

It is similar in approaching store buyers in that you must send them imagery, press releases etc, but if they love what you are doing &

feature or use your clothes in a spread shoot, then this is priceless exposure and fantastic brand building.

All independent boutique buyers travel globally in order to search out designers & lifestyle products for their stores, everything from fashion & accessories to scented candles, furniture and art. Having a point of difference is a major attraction for boutique buyers. As well as stocking established designers, they love to discover emerging talent not stocked by many.

When you are approached or you approach stores, try not to give total exclusivity. I allow a 15-20 mile radius between boutiques for exclusivity. That does not work in major cities. In London for example I may have 4 or 5 stockists all within a 10-15 mile radius. This is acceptable if the collection is popular with buyers but be careful not to supply stores too close to each other.

Once the collection becomes popular and strong, you cannot limit yourself to only one stockist per area. You will never grow this way and buyers being buyers will always try to push for exclusivity. You must weigh up a few things. Look closely at the store themselves and the size of order they intend on placing with you. If a particular boutique has placed a reasonably sized order and booked throughout the collection which will give you a greater exposure of the entire collection within their store then you must support this retailer over others. Better to be sensible initially rather than overexcited.

Make show cards & look books available to buyers, which we refer to as point of sale material, when you do finally deliver merchandise to them. Depending upon the imagery you hold and whether or not the images belong to you or the photographer (you must check this) showcards are usually done by the PR or us in house. This will go a long way with the buyer and show that you are not merely trying to take an order from them but are also prepared to help promote your goods in their store and drive custom to their tills.

Buyers do not have great loyalty anymore for obvious reasons and if the goods do not sell they, understandably, will move on. Do not take it for granted that once they buy they will continue to do so indefinitely.

If the goods do sell well and they come back the following season with a larger order, you should build upon this relationship.

When in a situation like I have had, whereby I had to choose between Browns Focus of London, a renowned independent chain of boutiques, or Selfridge's department store, then you must weigh up all odds. Remember department stores have even less loyalty if the sell throughs on a given collection are low and they also now ask for large discount terms, which they call settlement terms, in order just to deal with them. They also tend to display your goods by leaving it hanging on a rail with no specific salesperson to sell it. This is why I tend to support boutique business. They have a much more personalized approach, will help the consumer to any extent and will support the designer more so going forward. Department store business I see as a bonus, independent boutique business is the way forward. I chose to support Browns Focus by the way which proved the right decision.

Of course the larger orders can come from the department stores but if you fail to have a good sell through for no reason of your own, then you could be dropped after a single season and you may have messed up your chances of supplying the smaller independent boutiques at the outset because they will probably know that you were stocked by the department store and will possibly not want to be judged as second choice now you no longer have the support of the department store. Do not be blinded by wanting to be stocked primarily in the Likes of Selfridges or Harvey Nichols, it can, and often does, backfire. Build your customer base first, support independent boutiques, department stores will find out and approach you and then you will be in a far greater position to negotiate terms.

Department store buyers also check out the boutiques for emerging talent. It is a part of their job to keep an eye on the competition.

Target a small number of retailers initially but mail out to everyone. The best UK stores are all in my directory at the rear of the book. Exhibit within trade shows, if that option is available to you. This is the best way of taking initial orders as buyers will be able to view your collection en masse. This is where the mail out you do is invaluable so it must be effective & you must ensure it does gets read. You want buyers to make a beeline to your stand rather than exhibit in blind hope.

Do all of this in-house before approaching any agent, showroom or distributor. Later in the book I will discuss, in greater depth, the role of agents, showrooms and distributors. Fashion & newspaper press will be more interested in your collection if you can name drop retailers of your collection.

Always mail out to department store buyers but do not pin your hopes for orders here initially. Have a small number of boutiques that you will follow up with, say 30 -40 and make your calls and subsequent follow up calls to these stores. These are the ones you really would like your collection stocked in so pursue them without overly hassling them. Do not call 3 or 4 times a week.

Send them your best press and imagery, call and nurture them. Eventually they will agree to see you but only if they believe your collection may fit in with their product mix. Once in the store your only goal is to come out with an order. Even if you leave the store with interest for next season, you have not failed.

Never talk about minimum orders to a buyer even though they will ask. Always be vague! Always say to them, 'We don't actually have a minimum order, although we really can't ship out less than 30-40 pieces'. This will keep them interested. 30 pieces to a buyer represents a small order & will not break their bank, they don't know our wholesale prices exactly as of yet, so to us this could be a nice size order in value terms. Buyers never usually stick to their budgets anyway. If they love something, they always find budget for it and always end up buying more than the initial 30 piece minimum we asked for.

Boutique buyers will talk in payment terms and department store buyers will talk in settlement terms. Boutiques will expect to be offered standard payment terms, usually 30days net or 5% 7 days, whereby you expect to receive payment of your invoice within 30 days, or 7 days net 5%, whereby you grant the store a discount of 5% if they pay you

within 7 days. These are standard payment terms. Sometimes we extend this to 14 days but rarely.

When we deal with a totally new store that has recently opened, we often request a proforma payment whereby we will only deliver the order after the store has issued payment in full and funds have cleared into our account. We usually do this for new retailers who are just starting up and unable to provide trade references. Generally we will request a deposit of between 30-50% of the order value from the store prior to ordering cloth and commencing production. This is a better solution however not all retailers will agree to it. If a new store cannot meet our payment requirement, we decline the order. We are not in the business of taking undue risks.

Department stores all have their own settlement terms which differ greatly from store to store. Department stores take a much higher discount. For example, a given department store may state that they take 12% in settlement terms. This means they break down the 12% discount in any number of ways.

They may take 5% as a standard payment term discount, they may take a further 5% discount to allow for distribution, whereby you deliver to a single distribution centre and they subsequently deliver to all of their individual department stores nationwide thereby saving you the cost, and they may take what they call a retrospective discount, whereby they take a further 2% discount to allow for garments which go into their sale. Garments they are unable to sell at full price and therefore take a lower profit margin on these pieces.

When dealing with department stores, always ask upfront what their settlement terms are. If you develop business with any department store, ensure your profit margins allow for such discounts they take. Generally their settlement terms are non negotiable but that is not cast in stone as I have negotiated better settlement terms with department store buyers. It really depends upon how interested they are to stock the collection.

Chapter 4

How important is your paperwork?

The paperwork you maintain is vital, without accurate documentation you will find that fashion buyers will become highly frustrated when dealing with you and inevitably leads to late payment of invoices.

I appreciate that many will already have full understanding of the importance of documentation; this is for those emerging labels that are uncertain.

The following is a brief outline relating to important documents you will need when supplying boutiques & department stores on a wholesale basis.

- The delivery note.
- The invoice.
- The returns note.
- The credit note.

Aside from your order sheets, the above documentation is of great importance as there will be occasion where you deliver merchandise and the retailer calls you with queries.

The process for taking orders from and subsequent delivery and invoicing to department stores is very different than delivering and invoicing boutiques; therefore you must ensure that you adhere to the very specific requirements set out by department stores. They will very often have specific requirements for garment labeling & kimballing, packaging, swing tagging and bar coding.

They will provide you with full shipping, delivery and invoicing requirements and you must follow them precisely. Department stores will issue you with a purchase order when placing orders with you. This will not happen at the same time as you are writing the order with them. It is computer generated and sometimes takes weeks to come to you after the initial order has been written by you. Once received, this forms a contract and you must check each detail extremely carefully as buyers make errors also.

The delivery note.

The delivery note can be a duplication of your order sheet. It follows the same format; instead of calling it an order sheet just rename it to read 'Delivery Note'.

The delivery note must be placed in an envelope and be in the box with the goods you are shipping to the customer. On this delivery note you should write in detail, as you would write an order, the complete details of what is contained within. The style number(s), descriptions, sizes & colours. You can also put wholesale prices on the delivery note if you wish but it is not vital. When the shop staff take delivery of your merchandise they will use your information on this sheet to book the delivery in and check the stock in the box to the delivery note. They usually attach the checked off delivery note to the invoice. If there are any discrepancies between your delivery note and the garments in the box, the store will call you immediately as they do not want to be invoiced for pieces not received. Sometimes errors are made when the goods are picked and packed and a piece may not be placed in the box, this will make the delivery note inaccurate and the store will call you immediately. Sometimes, goods are stolen in transit by couriers. It is vital to enclose an accurate delivery note with your merchandise. The delivery note pad should be in duplicate or triplicate allowing for a copy for your records, a copy for the customer and a floating copy.

The Invoice.

The invoices you produce are usually computer generated and clearly a copy must be kept for yourself both on your computer and a hardcopy within the customers file. The invoice is also placed with the merchandise in the box in its own envelope. When the delivery is received by the store, the enveloped invoice will be passed to the buyer. Once the delivery is checked off by store staff they will pass the delivery note to the buyer who will cross check it to the invoice and attach the two together. The buyer will cross check all details on the invoice to the order sheet to ensure styles, prices, colours & quantities are the same. They will also cross check the payment terms you quoted at the time of writing the order.

The invoice will then be filed until its due date. This is often done both manually and on computer. It is very important to place an invoice with the merchandise because the invoice becomes due for payment once the goods are received by the store.

We also tend to send an invoice to the customer in the post. This really is to cover ourselves in case the invoice within the box becomes misplaced, which it often does! We address the invoice to the buyer directly; it is up to the buyer to pass the invoice to the relevant person who pays invoices, which with boutiques, can be the buyer/owner themselves but can also sometimes be a third party such as an outside accountant.

The returns note.

If a store wishes to return merchandise to you for any reason, they will require a returns note from you. This is a sheet of paper, similar to an order sheet, which outlines the date, style details, colour, size, quantity and also states the reason why the style(s) are being returned. This documentation is important for both retailer and supplier. It ensures that the goods have been returned by a store on a specific date and for good reason. Often we speak with stores beforehand to see if we can overcome the need to return merchandise. In the cases where we cannot, we must issue a returns note for the retailer.

The returns note is also important because often, on our terms & conditions which feature on the rear of order sheets, we state that merchandise cannot be returned after a specific amount of time has passed, usually 7 - 14 days. This allows the retailer to check the merchandise for damages or problems once received. Often this does not happen and retailers will simply hang the merchandise in store.

Problems are often only noticed when customers try the merchandise on. This can occur way passed our 7-14 day deadline. When situations such as these arise it is time to negotiate with the stockist. We obviously do not want to alienate our buyer(s) so we try to come to the best arrangement possible, sometimes we replace damaged pieces with perfect pieces, other times we swap styles completely. Either way, the store returning or swapping merchandise will want a returns note in order to keep their paperwork accurate. They are multi-brand retailers and these issues can arise across many brands in a given season. Buyers are notorious for keeping accurate paperwork, so must you be.

The credit note

If no arrangement can be reached with your retailer and they are adamant that they wish to return merchandise and there are no alternatives for replacing stock or swapping stock, we must issue a credit note once the merchandise has been received back to us and checked by us.

The credit note takes the same form as an invoice; it is merely renamed 'Credit note'. Again it is usually computer generated and therefore copies must be kept in the same manner as invoices are kept.

A credit note issued to a retailer for merchandise returned allows them to deduct the financial amount stated on the credit note from the invoice you have sent them. If you delay in sending your customer a credit note they are expecting, they will not issue payment to you against your invoice.

It is important that once the returned merchandise is received and checked by yourselves that a credit note is issued to the retailer involved immediately.

I have had many situations whereby invoices had become due and I have been calling the retailer chasing payment only to be told that a credit note is outstanding therefore the invoice would not be paid until received.

Ideally we do not want to be issuing either return notes or credit notes however situations beyond your control do arise and there will be circumstances where you will be left with no choice.

Ensure your documentation is organized beforehand and that you are not rushing around trying to buy or prepare a returns book or credit note book should a situation arise.

Pre-empt situations and become proactive and not reactive. The retailer in question will be appreciative of your diligence and will recognize that if problems do arise you are fully prepared to handle such issues. This will give them greater confidence in dealing with you going forward.

Every brand has returns issues from retailers, it is the nature of the business so do not take it personally just handle it with full professionalism and the likelihood is that you will still do business with the store in question going forward.

Chapter 5

The Exhibition Space, Showroom Space Trade-off

In my opinion, it is far more effective to show a collection within a showroom environment rather than in a store. This is because within your showroom you have the undivided attention of the buyer(s) and if they are there in the first place, it shows intention & willingness on their part.

A downside to presenting collections within a standalone showroom, as opposed to agent owned showrooms, is the related costs involved. If we are presenting two main collections a year, for a selling period of 8-10 weeks per selling period, it makes little sense committing to a long term lease that can tie you into a rental period of anywhere between 3-5 years and upward. Clearly there would be long periods between selling seasons where the showroom would not generate sales. This is money wasted. Better to seek short term lets for your selling season and rent showroom space only for your selling season. A lot of the larger estate and property agents have a glut of space waiting to be filled and some will be happy to rent on short term leases.

In central London for example, I can short term rent showroom space for roughly £85 per day which is a much more cost effective solution.

When renting showroom space, ensure that you are within an area that is suitable and convenient for buyers to visit. There is little point in renting a beautiful space in the middle of nowhere; you will find buyers will not take the risk of visiting you because they need to ensure that if your collection is not suitable for them, that they are just a short journey to the next showroom. Always ensure that wherever you plan to show from, it is located relatively close to other fashion showrooms and has good transportation links.

When contemplating showing your collection from a trade exhibition, ensure you have done as much homework on the exhibition prior to applying for space. Check the exhibitors listing to ensure like for like brands are exhibiting. Check the various area's within the show to ensure your product category is well represented and also check the competitive exhibitions which will be running alongside.

If budgets are tight and your decision has to be based upon either renting showroom space or exhibition space in your early seasons, I would opt for exhibition space every time. Why? Because buyers will visit these exhibitions en masse and there is no guarantee you will secure showroom appointments despite your best efforts and intentions.

There is nothing worse than sitting in a showroom waiting for a buyer to arrive. Buyers often double book appointments, run late, forget or just do not turn up. As an emerging brand it is harder to have buyers commit to a firm appointment, however if exhibiting at a relevant show, we are at least guaranteed walk past buyers. Our intention at shows is to have buyers visit our stand and we target aggressively prior to the exhibitions.

You can use an exhibition as a showroom for the duration of the show. Make appointments with buyers for them to visit you on your stand. Some buyers will and some buyers will not, it's the nature of the game, however it is prudent to do so regardless of whether you have uninvited buyers on your stand which may conflict with an appointment you have made. Far better for you to be overbooked and busy writing orders!

If buyers turn up to your stand whilst you are busy presenting, this actually helps, as it serves to show that your products are interesting. It always helps to have at least two salespeople on your stand at any one time for this very reason.

Regardless of whether showroom or exhibition space, you have to make best use of this expense. Your brochure or postcard mail out has to be effective and you must generate as many appointments as possibly. It really is a numbers game as not every buyer that views your collection will buy.

The right trade exhibition can have a tremendous effect on your selling season. If you select the exhibition wisely, you can generate more sales than a season of visiting retailers on the road. It is a great vehicle for writing orders however, if you are not active in inviting buyers to your stand prior to the show commencing and leave it to the off chance that they will be there anyway and will see your merchandise, you could be in for a very big shock.

Trade exhibitions feature prominent designers and brands. Some are well established whilst others are new. Most professional salespeople & agents in the industry would have fixed firm appointments on stand and will be seeking to attract new business to their stands. They would have been calling & emailing aggressively at least 6 weeks prior to the show. They will continue doing this right up until the day of the show and will continue doing so even whilst at the show.

Trade exhibitions are expensive and we have to ensure that they are commercially viable. This means we must write orders at the show and more specifically, we are searching for new business to complement our existing business.

Do your research both on relevant short term showroom space and trade exhibitions. Check with your local Department of Trade & Industry or relevant official body, they will be able to direct you to any grants that may be available to you to assist in covering the various costs.

Unless very centrally located and with beautiful spacious premises, do not attempt to show your collection from your home office or studio as I have. It can leave the wrong impression!

Chapter 6

Getting Paid

There is little point in us taking orders if we don't get paid by the boutiques & department stores we supply. They may take so long to pay us that we struggle to continue and finance future collections or even current samples & production. We do everything in our power not to take undue risks and to ensure that whoever we supply is able to pay on time.

New UK laws state that as suppliers, we are entitled to charge interest at 8% above the Bank of England base rate for late payers but how many of us actually do this? What easier way to lose an otherwise good stockist who may be suffering cash flow issues at the moment, there are alternative solutions and efficient strategies to ensure prompt payment.

One of the most important things to remember is to always have buyers sign your order sheets, which must have certified terms & conditions printed on the back. I have provided an example of T&C's later in the book. A lot of companies elaborate on T&C's. Buyers tend not to read them but if problems do arise you need to be fully covered. This does happen so ensure you are fully protected from the outset.

Most orders written are usually based on industry standard payment terms, which are 30 days net or 5% 7 days. This means if the store pays you within 7 days of invoice then you grant them a curtsey 5% discount for prompt payment.

With regards to the payment terms you state to any potential stockist, ensure that these terms are firmly in your favor. If you are approached by a new business with little credit history, it is prudent to ask for a non refundable deposit against the order (between 33-50%) with the balance to be paid on pro-forma terms. This means that before you order fabric to produce the order received from this new business, you would have received approx 50% of the invoice value against that order. You can now commence production. Once production is complete, a call is made to the customer to request balance payment before shipment. Once all monies are received and cleared funds into your bank account are you able to release the goods for delivery.

With new businesses it is better to be safe than sorry. You cannot apply for trade references as they will have none therefore you cannot decide whether they are credit worthy or not at the beginning. After a few seasons of them having developed a relationship with you and tracking their proforma payment history with you, will you be in a better position to judge and possibly offer them credit terms.

This does not relate to department store business. They have their own settlement terms which will vary from store to store but expect settlement terms to range anywhere between 10 and 15%. This means you have to be careful when doing business with the department stores. You must know beforehand their settlement terms. Don't be afraid to ask the buyer these terms as she/he is looking through your collection. They expect to be asked. Their terms are always on their purchase orders they provide when confirming an order with you.

Most stores, including department stores, take longer than the agreed 30 days to pay. In today's economy it's just the way it is. Cash flow is tight for everyone, so expect more realistic terms of payment to be anywhere between 45/60/90 days.

You will only get paid on time if you chase your invoice. Chase a few days prior to it becoming due so everyone can get the necessary documentation together. Buyers often misplace invoices, have incorrect bank details to send payment to or send out cheques when they should pay by telegraphic transfer so it is always wise to pre-empt these queries.

Prior to the invoice becoming due for payment, do all you can within your power and budget to help the store sell your merchandise. Sell through is king and if your sell through is high, come the day the invoice is due, the buyer will know and you will get paid. If your sell through is low come invoice due date, they will stall but this stalling will greatly depend upon what efforts you have made to assist in store sales of your merchandise.

This is where PR and creating hype really does help. It helps to drive customers both to their store and more importantly, toward your goods within their store. If buyers see this happening, even if your sell through is relatively low, come invoice due date, you will find you will get paid sooner rather than later.

With regards to the use of a factoring company, I personally have used them once and will probably not use this route again. They basically work like this. You provide them with your order book or entire invoices due for all of the shipments you have made to retailers. They pay you the amount due against all of your invoices less the commission they charge, which can vary anywhere between 5% - 10%. The benefit to you, immediate access to funds less the commission payable.

It is now in the interest of the factoring company to recover the amounts due from the retailers you have supplied and they want this done in the shortest time possible and they will use many methods to ensure they do so.

Often these methods differ from the methods you would employ to chase debt and do not sit comfortably with the buyer. This can be disturbing to your customer when constantly hassled and sometimes even threatened with legal action. This in turn can lead to the buyer not buying from you again in order to avoid this, so a word to the wise here. By all means use a factoring company but ensure you know whom they represent first and what their policy is for chasing and recovering debt.

It may be prudent to pay a little more in commission to them if they use a more understanding and lenient approach when chasing your retailer. Last thing you want is to lose a stockist based on how a factor speaks to them about invoices due or overdue.

Chapter 7

The Fashion Calendar

It is quite important to understand retail delivery patterns in the UK as buyers are often changing how they stock their shops to fit in with greater expectations from the customer and the changing, ever developing retail patterns. This is typical not only within the UK but worldwide.

There are still the two main fashion seasons but some designers are now showing up to 4/5 collections a year. Also, it has become ever more popular for buyers to buy merchandise in season. This type of buying is from short order collections; these collections typically deliver every 4 -6 weeks. It is a great way for the retailers to replenish their shelves & rails and keep on top of current and fast moving trends. It also helps retailers with their cash flow & budgeting forecasts.

More & more designers are offering multiple collections per year. You will always have the main Spring/Summer & Autumn/Winter collections, but there are also transitional collections, referred to as cruise or mid season collections.

Sales dates for Cruise/pre season collections vary slightly but generally S/S cruise collections are sold in late may/early June for delivery in store end October/early November. A/W cruise collections are sold in late October/Early November for delivery in store late may/early June.

Forward ordering is still the most popular way that buyers stock mainline designer collections; however in season buying is becoming ever more popular, hence short order collections are now doing great business. Unless your production capabilities and financing are secure and proven I would recommend sticking initially to producing two main collections per year initially for forward order.

Producing short order collections means constant sampling of new styles/colours in order to consistently show to buyers. This is not as easy as it sounds initially and requires a strong and sound financial background as well as capable production and sampling systems.

Not all buyers buy in season merchandise, some prefer forward ordering alone. Others mix the two and hold back budget for short order collections and in season buying.

Timing of sales is all important. Little point in coming out with a collection when buyers have spent all of their seasonal budgets or when they are preparing for in stores sales.

Familiarize yourself with the buying pattern for your country. Do not go by exhibition dates as these can be misleading. If not sure, ask a few key retailers when they buy for specific seasons.

Start buying, or subscribe to, two major trade press publications. They are 'Drapers' and 'Womenswear Buyer' or WWB. They can both be found online at www.drapersonline.com and www.ras-publishing.com. Both these publications outline everything that is current, from a trade perspective, in the UK fashion industry.

You cannot buy these publications over the counter unless you are based around the square mile in the heart of the fashion business in London W1. Just subscribe to them online, they are both well worth the money and will inform you about everything from exhibitions to new store openings.

Chapter 8

Production, QC, CMT make prices & fabrication costs.

A major issue facing emerging designers and brands is that of production & fabric costs. This is why I recommend that initially you stick to producing two main collections a year until such time as your production base is proven and your fabrication prices are workable. Also you must ensure that you are being paid on time by retailers before you can start producing more than two collections per year.

Unfortunately, most factories/CMT outworkers will charge you a premium for producing short production runs and samples. Fabric suppliers may also charge you a premium if purchasing an amount of cloth from them less than their minimum amount stated. They all have minimums. Some will not supply less than their stated minimums.

The solution is to take enough wholesale orders from retailers to ensure you meet the minimums requested by both the CMT unit and fabric suppliers. In the real world unfortunately sales on some styles can be low therefore we struggle to achieve the minimums requested. In cases where we know we are not selling a specific fabric story very well, we may drop the style or the entire story in that fabrication and push sales on other fabric groups which are selling better. We do not get personal with styles which we may personally love if the group is not selling well; better to cut it early than have a major problem later on.

When we are doing our costing sheets (See costing sheet example rear of book) which provides us full style information to enable us to arrive at a sensible wholesale price, we choose at this point to either use the higher factory price, premium included or the lower price without premium. It depends upon the style and the experience and confidence of the salesman/woman.

If he/she believes the style will be a good seller based on previous sales experience of similar styles, then it makes sense to use the lower make price given by the CMT factory as we can be confident in hitting the

minimum amount the factory will require to make it, which is referred to as the cutting docket given to the factory. It will also allow us to achieve a sensible wholesale price using lower costs involved in producing the style.

If the salesman is uncertain, better to play safe and opt for the higher CMT price given by the factory. If sales on a particular style are really low, we usually cancel the style completely and inform the few retailers that have ordered the style that it will not be made. We do not produce anything with either very low quantities or small profit margins involved.

It is important that when we are calculating and completing our costing sheets to enable us to put a wholesale price to a style, that we have done our homework prior and negotiated the very best fabric price we can get and the very best CMT price we can get. From this information we can calculate our best wholesale price and subsequent RRP.

If the CMT unit states that they require from you a minimum of 100 pieces per style in order to achieve the price they are giving you then you must also get a price if you were to give them an order of half of that, say 50 pieces. The CMT unit will put their price make up accordingly. This means they are charging you a premium for making less than they would like to. In factories, prices are based on the amount of time it takes to go through their production lines, they can easily produce 500 pieces in the same amount of time it takes them to produce 50.

You must advise your sales people of the minimums you need to achieve in order to produce. It is then up to the salespeople to 'push' that style. It is the same for fabric. They will also charge you a premium if you buy from them a lesser amount than their minimum. Again the salespeople should be aware so they in turn can 'push' specific cloths. Some fabric suppliers will not ship less than the minimums they state per cloth and you must know this before any sales campaign.

Try not to use a sample CMT unit for production. They are used to making samples and work a lot slower than true CMT units therefore your make price from these sample units will always be on the high side.

Better to have your showroom samples made by either yourself or a sample machinist whilst ensuring that when these samples are then passed to a CMT unit for production that they are able to reproduce your initial samples. This comes down to the patterns and instructions and can take some working through with a factory as it will be made in a very different manner than how you or a sample machinist put it together.

You will find that in most cases, CMT units will try to simplify the production of the style. This is where the experience of the designer and production person is very important. Usually, tweaks are made to a style to ensure easy production in a CMT unit. If not done carefully this can change how the style looks completely so it is a balancing act between the designer being happy with the final sample, the salesman being happy that what he has presented in the showroom is pretty much the same as to what is being produced in the factory and finally the factory being satisfied that they are able to produce what is required of them in a commercial manner.

The entire process depends upon many samples being made, tweaked and finally approved by all. These are called sealing samples.

Good CMT units are not easy to come by. See who they are working with, take a look at their quality and at their machinery. Good CMT units will always have cutting dockets in production (these are orders they are producing for other labels) and always be relatively busy. Find out what they are good at and what they are not good at. Do not give your beautiful Silk Chiffon dress to a maker whose main business is tailoring. They will, unintentionally, ruin your fabric!

Always check and re-check your fabric costings. Garment costings are calculated in cloth quantity, trimming amounts; make price and much more. Refer to my example provided at the rear of the book.

Allow 10% extra on everything when delivering to a factory. Buttons and tickets get lost and there can be fabric damages. This is the full amount of cloth you give to a CMT unit. If your costings are too generous, they will have excess fabric left over (which they call cabbage) and most, not all, will either make this up in garments and invoice you for the over makes or worse, keep the over makes and sell these them themselves to market traders. This happens so your fabrication costings must be accurate. If you under deliver fabric to a CMT unit they will call you immediately when the fabric is being laid to be cut. They will also call you if the fabric comes up narrower than you have stated or contains damages or shading on the rolls. You must work very closely with your CMT unit. Production is vital!

Quality control is just as vital and the only way to do a proper QC job is to both inspect production whilst it is happening and then to spot check production once it is finished.

Do not commence production on your garments without having had a sealed sample, or samples, from your CMT unit. A sealed sample is one that has been checked over by either yourself or your production department to ensure absolutely everything is correct as per your initial sample.

Check your garments specs, all measurements and allowances. Check the fit, make amendments if necessary then request a further sealing sample. Do not allow your expensive bulk fabric/material to be cut for production until you have signed off the sealing sample. Better to have 10 sealing samples made prior to production and get it right.

Also, be aware that CMT units sometimes like to make 'suggestions' to better your design on your behalf. They are doing this to simplify their production processes and make their job faster and easier and more cost effective for themselves however it could, and often does, change the style beyond all recognition. Buyers will see this and will return the style to you. Work closely with your QC, salesman and CMT unit to ensure that if any tweaks or adjustments are made that they do not change the look and finish of the style completely.

QC starts from the moment the style is being sold by the salesman. At that time production staff and QC's are working on producing the style in the quantity the salesman finally sells.

Sometimes, we have to change or substitute the fabric the original sample came in. This happens for a multitude of reasons. Sometimes the fabric supplier will have problems producing the cloth and cannot deliver the original fabric we sampled our style in. This is not ideal but does happen. If the fabric is completely different to the selling sample we must inform and show the buyers and hope they do not cancel. Often they will cancel. If the fabric is only a very slight change in colour variation, we do not inform the buyers. If the fabric composition changes, you must inform the buyers.

This is all picked up by production & QC and told to us as salespeople in the frontline between them and the buyers. It is up to us to ensure we do not get cancelled orders. Sometimes it is better to cancel a complete style if the fabric is unavailable rather than try to 'substitute' a fabric and hope to get away with it. This is usually a very expensive error on our part. Better to take a small loss in orders rather than a huge loss trying to substitute a cloth or fabric, without informing your retailers.

Buyers have an uncanny memory when it comes to merchandise they have ordered and they will know and they will return the entire style. You would have lost not only the fabric/production/ shipping costs plus associated profit margins but also be left with unwanted pre-sold stock.

Seal all of your samples multiple times if necessary. Ensure all samples are 100% accurate prior to starting production. Do not substitute fabrics or materials and hope to get away with it.

You or your QC must spot check production whilst it is going through the factory and randomly spot check production once it is finished. Then and only then are you ready to have your merchandise picked and packed ready for shipping to your wholesale customers complete with any point of sale material you may have such as brochures or showcards.

A word about profit margins. We all work on different profit margins which must be maintained. It is easy to sell merchandise for little profit but extremely risky. No matter how stunning a style may appear, if it is not cost effective to produce, drop it from the collection. Most designers I have worked with will not attempt to sell a style within their collections for less than a 50% gross profit margin and often only focus on styles achieving them a 100% profit margin or greater. This makes perfect sense as you may not sell a huge quantity in your early seasons so better to capitalize by using a higher margin at the outset. Profit rules not turnover.

Production, fit and quality is what you will be judged on when your goods are delivered to retailers. If your showroom samples differ greatly from your final production and you deliver this to retailers, expect problems.

Ensure that you have correctly fitted your initial samples and that your fits work. There is little point in delivering a stunning looking jacket that nobody can buy because the armholes are too tight or the sleeve length too long. Fits are extremely important and are often an expensive after thought. Your fits must be perfect before you give your final patterns and graded size sets to a factory. If you do not do this you will be asking for a very expensive problem.

Chapter 9

Design

Fashion & Accessory designers create from the heart & from their inspirations. As you will read about further in the book, recommended retail prices are key therefore your wholesale & RRP prices must be competitive & attractive and also sit alongside the other established designers the particular retailer is stocking.

An important factor for designers to bear in mind, without compromising design flair, is the cost of the fabrics & materials selected to use and the ultimate make price the factory will charge to produce the style.

If you, as the designer, select a fabric or material at say £40 per meter and decide to use 2 meters of that fabric in a given style, by the time you add all the other associated costs (production, trimmings, commissions, duty, shipping and your profit margin) you may arrive at a completely unrealistic wholesale and retail pricepoint and possibly the style may not sell for this reason, however it does depend on your particular market sector.

My only advice here is to be sensible in your fabric or material selection and if using expensive materials, keep your costings workable to make the wholesale price achievable, that way, as salespeople, we have a much higher probability of selling that specific style.

When we look at the collection as a whole, some prices work out at fantastic value for money whilst others appear overly priced.

We look at every costing sheet per style individually and see where we can raise the wholesale price of one style to compensate for us lowering the wholesale price of another. Your profit margin is vital and must be maintained overall.

When it comes to offering colour options, buyers tend to buy into what they can see so sometimes it is prudent to sample in multiple colours in order to sell those colour options.

We don't want to sample everything in every single colour otherwise our sampling costs would spiral out of control, however we careful go through the collection and we sample in relevant colours accordingly whilst maintaining a cohesive look through the collection. We do not want a 50 piece collection to turn into a 200 piece collection because we have sampled every style in every colour option.

We will carefully prepare our showroom look books which contain everything about the collection a fashion buyer would need to know to enable them to place orders. That would include fabric swatches of colour options available.

I have intentionally kept this chapter on design very brief as design is a very specific subject in itself and to be honest every designer has their own distinct signature or handwriting. As salespeople our efforts are based upon believing in designs we are given and offering opinions to our designers or design teams without compromising their flair.

Chapter 10

The collection is complete

Finally our designers have created and completed a beautiful sample collection and it is up to us, as salesmen & women, to take forward orders and have the collection stocked by the best retailers and e-tailers.

This in itself can be a challenge, as every designer wants the same thing, to be stocked in Selfridges, Harvey Nichols, Bloomingdales, Saks, Bergdorf, Neiman Marcus, Browns, Liberty, Matches et al therefore fashion buyers are swamped with information from designers around the world every season.

As salespeople, we have to be realistic and we have to know, before we approach fashion buyers, that our collection sits nicely alongside all the other designers they currently stock. Knowledge is important & gives us an edge when in conversation with a particular buyer as they prefer for us to have some kind of understanding about their business rather than blindly approaching them, which makes perfect sense.

Firstly, we do our research on the store and we find out who they are stocking and most important, what their retail price points are. We don't want to approach them with an unknown label if we appear overly expensive against the labels they stock or even too cheap. We must make sure that our pricing structure fits in nicely with the stores we are targeting and their product mix.

We tend to research either online, by phone call or by visiting the stores. This is called pre-season roadwork and is intensive and time consuming but very important if you are to really understand the nature of the retailer you are trying to do business with.

E-tailers, or on line retailers, are doing fantastic business which is growing seasonally. Most boutiques also have fully transactional websites. You must allow them to be able to sell your products online. Some of the biggest & brightest fashion e-tailers in the UK include the likes of Net-a-Porter, Mr Porter.com, ASOS and My wardrobe; however most boutiques and independent retailers also have fantastic online outlets which compliment their retail stores perfectly. Do not give any e-tailer total exclusivity; you will alienate boutique business if you give any e-tailer complete online exclusivity.

A correct pricing strategy is vital. There is little point an emerging designer trying to sit alongside an established designer at an even higher price point, again you may alienate the buyer. It makes better sense to research your market and make sure your designs are either at a competitive price or slightly lower than like for like designers already stocked. Although you may have complete confidence in your merchandise, a fashion buyer will be more hesitant and will view an emerging designer as un-tried and un-tested. They do not yet know what your fits & quality will be like, if you will deliver the order 100% without any shortages or damages and what the sell through on the shop floor will be like.

All buyers have cut their budgets due to the economy; however fashion buyers are always looking for that something different, that something fresh and that something which the press love & celebrities adore.

This is how we can score highly with buyers. If we have a collection that press, celebrities & buyers support, our job is made easier, in most cases we don't have the above so we need to create the hype & then supply the stores so they can in turn benefit from the hype created.

Under normal circumstances this is done by hiring a PR to both create the hype around the brand for us via press releases, editorials and product placements in related publications. The problem is that PR's can be expensive and without retailers stocking your collection the press on the whole will not give your merchandise any product placement space within their publications if they cannot quote a stockist or two, with contact details, to direct their readership to.

To create hype and brand build it is important to exhibit at tradeshows such as Pure London, Stitch menswear, London Fashion Week, Coterie in New York, Designers & Agents NY, Tranoi in Paris, or White in Milan. It is very important that you showcase your designs to the right audiences as buyers do talk to one another and spread the word organically. It will also offer you the best possible chances to secure either orders or appointments for the future.

I would steer away from fashion agents/distributors and showrooms in your very first season if you are new or trying to break into the market initially without any PR.

What will probably happen is that an agent may take your collection because they believe they can do good business with it, but what tends to happen, in the early seasons especially, is that buyers visit the showroom, primarily for the established designers these agents represent, they book those collections first and they may or may not browse over your collection.

If fortunate, you may get an initial small trial order if the buyers really like what they see. In my experience, it's doubtful 1st season to take multiple orders for a new designer with little hype behind the brand. Buyers sometimes do, but rarely these days, fall head over heels in love with a collection therefore it is a lot tougher these days to secure orders.

Sometimes everything does come together, the prices are great, the styles and fabrications are great and the agent or showroom do take initial orders on a new collection with little or no PR behind it. I have done this myself many times, however it is so much easier when there is a little hype behind the collection and buyers are actually seeking you to view the line they have read or heard about.

Chapter 11

Creating the hype

The question is how do you make your collection appealing to buyers and at the same time create hype around your label/brand/collection without a PR?

In order to find out the names of the relevant fashion editors and their assistants, do as I sometimes do. Buy the relevant magazines and they are listed inside then call to double check. Make initial contact with an assistant by email. Send them a fabulous image and a little background information about the designer/collection. If you have a press release, even better, email it to them.

Do not send them prior press you have received. They are not interested. Feature editors/assistants are interested in a story. Fashion editor/assistants are interested in product placement and fashion shoots. Magazines like to call off samples if interested so samples must be made readily available to them.

Often there is little to no budget available to us for advertising campaigns & marketing campaigns within the magazines. We cannot compete with the major brands as they spend fortunes on marketing and advertising. It's all to keep the momentum of the hype behind their brand so the spending public will continue buying that brand.

Celebrity endorsement is expensive. Unless a stylist can get a celebrity they are styling to wear your piece for free, it will cost you. Without advertising finances available to us, we must work hard to get product placement in magazines. It's a constant supply of samples selected by fashion editors & their assistants in the hope that one of our pieces will be used. You have little to no influence in their decision making.

Trade press is also a fantastic way of attracting retailers. 'Women's wear buyer' and 'Drapers' are two very important publications we target. Press does create hype, stylists can create hype, as fashion designers and as salespeople we utilize this exposure by making sure the buyers we are trying to attract get to see it.

When a designer I represent receives coverage in the press, I make sure all the buyers I want stocking the collection get to see the shot or editorial by mailing or emailing it to them.

If you do not have a PR, which most emerging designers do not, it falls to us to try to develop in-house PR. We have to try to entertain the fashion editors and in particular their assistants.

Their assistants will be the one's doing the donkey work on behalf of the editors, so these are the people we entertain initially until were in the door. Send them show invites, invite them to come see the collection, send pictures, images, look books, freebies! Gift them, call them, make them feel as if they are about to discover the next big thing & when they present their 'find' to their fashion or feature editors, they will feel that little bit special in having discovered you.

If we are able to secure product placements in the top magazines, job done. If we secure features on our designers, great job done. If we get both done, we ask for a rise!

Chapter 12

To e or not to e?

A question that often arises refers to e-tailing. I am often asked whether a designer should sell via their own websites or will that conflict with the transactional websites of wholesale clients.

It will only conflict if your recommended retails prices differ. I believe it makes great sense to have your own, fully transactional website, one where you actively sell your products online direct to your end customer. If you are also involved in wholesaling, you must ensure that recommended retail prices are adhered to otherwise you run the risk of confusing the customer and alienating your wholesale customers.

Also when it comes to PR product placement, it is prudent to list selected retailers as stockists rather than list your own website. This can infuriate retailers as they are seeking assistance in selling your products within their stores. They will not appreciate the direct competition from your own website.

When launching a transactional website it is important to be aware of costs involved. Not only the cost of design and implementation of the website alone and the hosting of the website, but the costs related to holding stock to supply the orders you receive from direct customers online.

The beauty about ordering online is the convenience, speed and ease it offers your customers; however be aware that online customers can be impatient and will want their purchase from your website delivered quickly. This means that in order to fill these online orders you have little choice other than to hold stock. This is where considerable costs can arise.

Depending upon your merchandise & online offer, you will have to cut stock without any pre-sales with a view to selling this stock online. This in itself can be risky. The disadvantage compared to traditional brick & mortar retailers who also have an online presence is that they will probably already have dedicated traffic visiting their website. Most boutiques create databases of customers that visit their stores, some take it many stages further and will know the exact sizes and preferences per customer. This means that they have the advantage initially with regards to internet traffic. They also are multi-brand stores so their offer will be more substantial than yours.

An advantage you have as a designer is the offer you are able to present to the customer regarding your collection. Most boutiques will not place an order for your entire collection, in fact they never do. They will have personal favorites from your collection and will select the pieces that they are confident will sell well for them both in store and online.

This usually means that a percentage of the collection does not sell at all, as once we see a style is underperforming we drop it from the collection to enable us to concentrate on the better selling styles. These styles that do not sell become unwanted samples, unless you have online representation yourself.

Now you are able to offer your consumers further styles that are not available via your stockists (because they never placed orders on them in the first place).

This enables you to showcase more of your entire collection online than anyone else. A major advantage for you, as fashion buyers are generally conservative when place first orders on a new collection. They dislike taking too many risks with their own money so are hesitant in placing orders for styles they are uncertain about.

If you want to showcase more of your collection, on your own fully transactional website, it means cutting more stock across more styles and greater cost outlay for you. It's a risk as you do not know the customers reaction to your merchandise, they may buy it, they may not and the last thing you want t is to be left with un-sold outdated stock.

What we tend to do is this. We take our forward orders from our stockists in the normal manner during the selling season. Once we have collated all our orders, it is very easy to see the best selling styles and colours. These are the styles & colours we shall also offer on our website. We shall also look closely at the styles that did not sell to stockists and from these we make an informed decision as to which styles to add in for online stock. Usually the decision is based on the price, style, fabrication and ease of production.

We do not cut very much stock initially, it's too risky in the early seasons, better to be conservative and sell out of it completely. Once you have an indication of what customers prefer, you can elaborate on your online offer later, but in your early days, do not take too many risks with regards to holding stock as you cannot be guaranteed of online sales at the outset.

So, to answer the question to e or not to e? The answers is yes, certainly develop a fully transactional website but with regards to your initial online offer, keep it tight and focused for the first season or two to reduce risk.

You will not discourage your retailers stocking your merchandise if you maintain RRP's throughout and you must utilize PR for your stockists.

If you advertise, which usually we do not have budget for, but if you do, by all means list your own website details as it is your ad, but when it comes to product placement, you should list and support your wholesale clients as you want to develop these accounts and not alienate them.

Chapter 13

Agents, Showrooms & Distributors

In your early seasons the hard work and legwork must be done by yourself and team before approaching agents, showrooms or distributors. If you have 5 or 10 good stockists and have delivered merchandise to them and received sell through sales data before approaching an agent, showroom or distributor, you will have so much more bargaining power when it comes to negotiations, and there are always commission negotiations to be discussed.

Agents, showrooms & distributors play a vital part in the growth of any designer or brand; however agents have to make a living also so prefer to represent collections they believe will give a good return for their time and effort. In the UK we regard third party salespeople as agents; in the US they are regarded as Showrooms, same difference. They are all agents if they earn commission from you. A distributor does not earn commission from you. A distributor would be classed as a sole customer to you in a specific territory.

If approached by 10 new designers a season, any agent will look at many different elements before coming to a decision. They will look at the potential of the collection, the price points and the background of the designer. They will also look closely at the financial stability and viability of the designer, the production capability, the quality of the samples, and the point of sale materials provided as well as any press generated.

Generally an agent will examine the structure of the business and whether you are new, established or highly spoken about. Agents are trying to figure out how easy or difficult it will be to sell the collection in depth to buyers and thereby create income in the form of commission generated.

Sometimes a designer may already supply a small handful of accounts in the territory they are asking the agent to cover. If this happens, be prepared to hand over these accounts to the agent as he/she will want to develop those accounts and therefore earn commission with them.

Occasionally specific accounts are handled by the designer or sales person who opened them and kept in-house, however, in most cases; these accounts are passed to the agent. This can be a sweetener for the agent concerned. If a large account, such as a department store, has been opened and developed by yourself, it is unlikely this account will be passed to any agent.

Agents typically charge anywhere between 10 - 15% commission. Some showrooms charge participation fees. This tends to be the case with showrooms in the US. They will expect a monthly contribution from you to cover costs. The amount varies from showroom to showroom and should always be negotiable.

Agents work on invoiced commissions. This means that you pay them a pre agreed commission rate, say 10%, of the amount you invoice to a retailer that the agent has opened and taken an order from. You do not pay commission on the order amount. The difference is, say an agent takes an order from a store and that order is valued at £5000 however when you come to shipping merchandise to that store, your invoice value is only £3000 due to shortages you may have, damages you cannot send out and the like, the commission you pay an agent would be 10% of £3000 and that would become payable to the agent 7 days after you have been paid by the store. Most designers and brands obviously try as hard as possibly to ship an order 100% complete however in many cases this does not happen.

Distributors will require a discount of anywhere between 20 - 35% off your normal wholesale price dependent upon the size of single bulk order they will give to you.

An important thing to remember about agents, showrooms and distributors. Although they may love what you are doing, they are a commercial business and must make money & that is primary for them. They may completely love your collection however primarily they are concerned with the income potential it may generate for them.

When working with a distributor, you are basically giving up control of your brand in the territory they cover. The distributor will be your sole customer. It is up to them where they place your goods.

For example, if you negotiate a deal with a distributor whereby they will place an order with you for say $100,000 and for this order they require 30% off wholesale price, they would have already pre- sold the collection, at full price, to individual retailers on their database therefore they will want a sample collection from you in order to do so. The 30% discount represents their profit margins and allows for shipping to their customers etc.

It can be a double edged sword in as much as you do not want to turn away the business of $100,000 as well as having stockists in a foreign territory; however you cannot also control the stockists the distributor then sells to and at what price.

The advantage of having a distributor is that they act as your sole customer. At the end of their selling season they will provide you with a single bulk order. This will reflect all styles and colours they have pre-sold and may also include a small amount added on for repeat orders they expect. You will deliver a single order to the warehouse of the distributor. They in turn are responsible for individually picking and re-packing and delivering the stock according to the orders they have from the stores they have supplied. They are responsible for invoicing their customers, delivery notes, credit notes and all relevant paperwork. Your responsibility is to supply bulk merchandise to the distributor as per his bulk order to you and receive payment from the distributor. Your payment terms with your distributor are usually negotiated prior to sending him the sample collection for him to pre sell.

Sometimes a distributor may negotiate with you shared control, where you do have a say in which stores they sell to and at what price, this will be reflected in the discount on wholesale price they ask for.

An agent or showroom will only wholesale your collection based on potential commission they may earn. They will push your collection if they stand to earn 15% commission or higher. The problem here is that as designers/exporters, you may try to cover these costs by costing in all the additional elements, commissions, shipping, duty if applicable etc, to your wholesale price. Your wholesale price could become too high and the merchandise does not sell in the showroom because the recommended retail price (RRP) will be too high for buyers so they shy away from placing orders with you.

Negotiate with the agent to take a smaller commission and attempt to bring your shipping prices down so you must get a good transportation deal at your end. If there is import duty to be paid, I advise you to add it into the wholesale price and recoup through your wholesale price. The correct terminology for this wholesale pricing strategy is called is Delivered Duty Paid (DDP).

Another reason to add in import duty, if it is applicable, to the wholesale price is because most, if not all, buyers get very confused having to work out their RRP based on your wholesale price without duty added. They also dislike receiving two invoices, one from you & the other from Customs. It becomes a mental barrier for them.

Buyers prefer things to be kept simple so tell them at the outset that there is no duty or shipping, & your prices are DDP; delivered duties paid, & guess what happens? They relax & you are much more likely to take an order. Simple but very effective & very true! I have taken many an order based on this. Keep delivery & shipping terms as simple as possible.

Quoting a DDP price means your wholesale price has to incorporate the cost of duty & shipping. Think of it as delivering from your door right to the customer's door and what it will cost you entirely. Your wholesale price, when quoting DDP terms, must allow for this. DDP is only applicable when delivering overseas into a country where duty is applicable.

FOB (Free on Board) is usually a price requested by department stores because their shipping departments can negotiate a far better rate of shipment than we can. Quoting a FOB price to a buyer will be lower than quoting them a DDP price because they are negotiating shipment once the goods reach a specific port.

CIF (Cost, Insurance and Freight) I doubt very much you will have much request for this type of payment term unless you are involved with shipping thousands of pieces to a given retailer such as Top Shop.

For a much greater insight into all Inco terms such as DDP, FOB, EX-WORKS, CIF, visit **www/foreigm-trade.com**

Keep your wholesale prices competitive & the agent or showroom will sell more, too high and they will struggle which means less orders for you.

A good agent will also be responsible for chasing invoices on your behalf. Agents are paid 7 days after the store has paid the designer so it is prudent for agents to supply stores known to pay well and on time.

We know the good paying stores from the bad. We try not to supply the bad no matter how beautiful!

If you are able to get a few stockists beforehand, you can show that there is a demand for your product and the agent, showroom or distributor will acknowledge that.

Any agent who asks for more than 15% commission is being greedy. This agent does not believe that he/she will sell a lot and is looking at risk to reward. They already know that they will have to expend greater time and effort at the outset and some agents/showrooms are reluctant to do that. Most agents prefer the easy sell and if offered a collection with an established customer base, will mostly give preference to this as opposed to new and emerging designers and brands with no established customer.

At the end of this book I have listed who I consider to be the top London agents and showrooms. Make approaches to them with the same consideration you would if approaching a fashion buyer. Agents and showrooms are very choosy with regards to which they represent; they have to be as it is their reputation on the line also.

Chapter 14

Why some labels succeed where others fail.

Having worked with so many designers and labels, I can assure you that the ones which succeed in the industry run a very tight ship. They keep expenses as low as possible and drive sales as much as possible. They ensure that every element that goes into the collection has been clearly thought through, right from the target price point and market sector, to the fabrication used and samples produced.

Prior to the collection being finalized, the sales & marketing campaign strategy for the season would already be underway, any exhibitions planned would have been researched and applied for in good time and they will know exactly what to expect in terms of sales budgets for the season. All marketing materials used in attracting buyers to the collection would have been sent and follow up calls will be a daily occurrence.

Sales people will be aggressively targeting prospective buyers with a view to arranging a viewing appointment. These prospective buyers would already have been vetted in terms of suitability for the collection being sold. This will happen anywhere from 6-8 weeks prior to the sales dates commencing.

With regards to production, every sample will have a costing sheet which clearly shows, in precise detail, every cost that will go into producing that style. It will show the net profit margin earned by wholesaling that particular style. Any style which did not meet exact criteria would already have been dropped from the collection. Only those styles which make commercial sense end up in the final collection which must maintain a cohesive look throughout.

Each piece or story within the collection would have been scrutinized with regards to fits, colour's available, sizes and prices.

Only when design, sales and production are in complete agreement will a collection be ready to present to buyers. All three departments work hand in hand.

Once the selling season is underway the production department, or person, is busy working with CMT factories having sealing samples produced. This can be a lengthy procedure but is vital. Occasionally during the selling season we may further drop styles from the collection if the sales are poor. We do this so we can focus the sales on stronger selling styles. This ensures that we shall sell a sufficient amount, in both quantity of style and fabrication.

At the end of the selling season, all orders are collated. From this information, everything required to make that quantity of style can be ordered. Fabrics, trimmings, labels, linings.

This is done for every single style and is further subdivided into specific amounts sold per colourway.

Production and quality is paramount to success and your production person or department has responsibility for this. It is their job to ensure that production sealer samples are exact in terms of quality and specification. They have to equal or exceed the quality of the selling sample presented to the buyers in the showroom.

Bulk production starts once production issue cutting dockets to the CMT units making the styles. Usually specialist factories make specific items therefore your production person may be working with 3-4 CMT units at any one time. Sealing samples will be requested from each unit making specific styles.

Once bulk production is underway, regular visits are made to the unit to ensure quality & standards.

You will not be judged by retailers on the professionalism shown in the showroom. You will be judged on the garments you deliver to them.

Whilst taking orders in the showroom you would have given the buyer a delivery date written on the order sheet. We usually give a commencement date and a completion date. This is because when our garments are in production, they often come from different factories, sometimes different countries and it will be difficult for us to confirm an exact date we can deliver goods in store.

Ideally we want to deliver all merchandise in one drop to the retailer so we will wait for all styles to be delivered to us from our CMT units before we can pick and pack all the styles ordered by a retailer before making delivery.

When delivering merchandise, everything must be perfect whether you are delivering flat packed in boxes or hung and pressed in hanging boxes.

We aim to have our merchandise delivered to our retailers in as pristine condition as possible so it is prudent to choose a reliable and efficient delivery service to do so. Do not use a courier who will throw your boxes around with little care. Research this area also as there are specific couriers who are experienced in the delivery of fashion merchandise. Everything is thought through carefully.

Within the box you should attach a delivery note with the merchandise and an invoice. Both should be clearly marked and be in separate envelopes. The invoice should be addressed to the buyer who placed the order.

We enclose them separately because when the goods are delivered to the store, they are often received by store staff and not the buyer. Store staff are sometimes required to check in the merchandise. In order to do so they will require a delivery note, this shall list in great detail, whatever merchandise is within that box. This delivery note is ticked off and attached to the invoice and passed to the buyer.

If you do not do this you may find discrepancies appear between what you say you have delivered and what the store say has been delivered. You must have a clear record of what you dispatch. If there are to be discrepancies you must ensure your paperwork is accurate. Discrepancies often happen.

Although we attach an invoice in the box, we also send an invoice in the post. This is to ensure that the buyer has the invoice! When it comes to getting paid on time we want to ensure that the paperwork is with the relevant person and has not been misplaced.

Credit control is one of the reasons some labels fail. You may have taken great forward order sales in the selling season and your production and quality of produced garments may be perfect. You may have delivered on time or even early and have given your retailer beautiful point of sale materials, such as window showcards, to help assist in the sale of your merchandise in store. You may be doing everything within your power from a PR standpoint, to help drive consumers to your product in store, but if you are not paid on time by your retailer you will struggle to continue.

It is vital to any new label that payment is made to you on time. In some cases you will have negotiated proforma payment terms or C.O.D payment terms. You may have taken a deposit beforehand from the retailer prior to ordering fabric and commencing production. All of this will help reduce risk on your part. If however you have given standard payment terms of 30 days net then it is up to you to ensure you are paid on time. It is inevitable in this retail climate that some retailers will pay later than the payment terms you granted. Chase, chase, chase! Work with your retailer, offer a payment plan whereby you are a paid a regular weekly amount. Retailers do this often as it helps their cash flow also. You will be in a better position if you take a smaller weekly payment rather than wait for your invoice to be settled in full.

I cannot stress enough the importance of credit control.

The reason some labels succeed where others fail all comes down to the planning and strategy involved prior to commencing the collection.

Before the design of a single sample you should have a clear understanding of your target market and how you intend to approach that market.

You should have a clear understanding of your sales & marketing strategy and the costs involved. You should be in a position to know which CMT units you have in mind to produce your collection and the costs involved. You should be fully aware of the requirements of your fabric suppliers.

Devise a potential sales budget and strategize against expected sales. How will you finance production should you achieve sales of 'X 'on your collection?

What will be your suggested payment terms to retailers? Will you ask for a deposit on all orders taken? What if they tell you they do not work like that, do you have a plan B? Will you offer them proforma payment or offer a payment plan to them?

Questions such as this need to be addressed prior to producing your sample collection. Designing a collection is the fun part where your creativity can run wild and so it should but with commercial restraints!

An understanding of the business of fashion is paramount for success.

I reiterate, the reason some labels succeed where other fail is in the planning. Plan for the best and worst case scenarios. Think through every element in your mind prior to designing a sample collection. Business plans are great but often, once written, they are filed away as we get excited about the prospect of launching a new label.

Well written business plans will not only save you a fortune but it will show clearly show whether or not your business idea is viable. It will alert you to the financial requirements needed to sustain the business as well as the day to day requirements.

Write a business plan and present it to advisors who are in a position to advise. Once your business plan makes commercial sense, only then should you contemplate wholesaling as it can be costly to do especially if your collection is very well received and you take many orders which will all require producing, which costs.

Chapter 15

Conclusion

Showroom sales, whether for clothing, accessories, bags, shoes, jewellery or swimwear, is no longer about pressure or volume selling; it is the art of persuasion in presenting.

The relationship between supplier and retailer has changed a lot. It is now more of a partnership than ever before. It is important to work alongside our retailers to ensure your products stocked sell well. Stock swaps are ever more common whereby if a certain style is not selling in store for whatever reasons we will swap that style for one which has performed better in store. This depends on levels of stock held at any one time.

Initially keep PR in house by doing it yourself in a scaled down version of what a PR would do for you. Gather the top selling fashion magazines and Sunday fashion supplements in the newspapers and find out, via the editorial pages, the details for the fashion & feature editors. Send them imagery and a press release, follow up with a phone call. Try to approach fashion stylists also. A great website which helps with mass emails is www.ymlp.com I have found that using these guys is simple, cheap and very effective. They also track which emails bounce, which are dead and which emails sent have been received and opened!

Ensure your collection is sensibly priced and that your subsequent recommended retail prices are relevant to the retailers being targeted.

Utilize both the buyer men's and women's directories at the rear of the book and develop your own directory. Mail all stores on your list. Follow up with a smaller set amount & send them your best imagery by post. Have a few of your key price-points indicated. Follow up with phone calls & attempt to make an appointment.

Once you have an appointment, your goal is to secure an order, so do ensure you know a little about the store & the designers stocked prior so that your wholesale prices will not cause the buyer to think twice.

Once writing order's, ensure your order sheets contain terms & conditions on the reverse. Set a minimum order in pieces and as far as possible stick to this.

If a style is not selling for any reason, drop it from the collection and focus on the styles that are selling better.

Always remember that some buyers will and some buyers will not place orders but always persevere. Buyers are a law unto themselves and change their minds often. Persistence and dedication always pays dividends in the end so never be swayed by the comments of others, always stick to & pursue you dream whilst accepting constructive criticism along the way, ultimately, you shall be as successful as the work you put in at the beginning

Planning is everything & each department compliments the other. Design, sales & marketing, production, credit control, dispatch & delivery all must work in tandem in order for long term success.

I hope I have managed to give you a far better insight into what is actually required to secure orders for your fashion and fashion related merchandise.

The fashion industry continues to expand, price points have become more and more competitive and buyers have an enormous choice from designers worldwide. Buyers love to discover something new & well priced and are always on the lookout for upcoming designers and brands that are not stocked everywhere. This fact alone makes you, as emerging new talent, highly desirable.

Success is everywhere, new & emerging designers and brands are being snapped up every season. Ensure you are presenting yourself in the best possible light as fashion buyers recognize great talent and will always support it.

As a final note, I would like to take this opportunity to wish you every success and remember, 'Successful people do the things un-successful people don't want to do'. (I repeat this to myself over and over every time I find myself having to do something I really cannot be bothered to do!)

Please feel free to drop me a line at mail@boutiquebuyers.com if you're stuck and in need of further help, also if you need a list of all the current fashion editors and assistant's, drop me a line anyway and I will email it to you as a freebie.

Kind Rgds
Renato

Examples & Explanations

Item	Quality	Width (cm)	Quantity	Unit Price	Total
Fabric 1	100% linen	160	2.5	$9.50	$23.75
Fabric 2	100% linen	160	0.5	$11.50	$5.75
Fabric 3					
Lining	100% silk	160	2.5	$4.00	$10.00
Fusing					
Shoulder pad					
Sleeve head roll					
Grading	Full size set			$2.00	$2.00
Buttons					
Zip	YKK 20cm nylon		1	$1.55	$1.55
H. Loop			2	$0.01	$0.02
Label	Centre back No.		1	$0.05	$0.05
Comp. label	Left side seam		1	$0.02	$0.02
Cost of materials					$43.14
Packaging.					$2.00
CMT make price					$30.00
Overheads	5%				$3.74
QA100	**BIAS SKIRT**			**Total Cost**	**$78.70**

This **costing sheet** example shows style **QA100** which is a bias cut skirt.

Explanation

There are two qualities of linen used and it is lined in silk. The total cost of linen used (fabric 1+2) is **29.50**, whilst the silk lining costs **10.00** in total. Our overhead costs cover us for things such as factory visits. You can choose to either add or deduct this cost.

After adding all sundry costs, style QA100 costs **78.70** to produce. This is before we add our profit margin.

If we were to add a 50% profit margin, the math would look like this:
78.70 x 0.50 =**39.35**
78.70 +39.35 = **118.05**

We would round this down to wholesale this style at **118.00**

Using a typical UK retail markup of 2.8, this style would retail for **330.04 (118x 2.8)** this would be rounded down to retail at **330.00**

This skirt would cost us **78.70** to produce
We would wholesale the skirt for **118.00 (Unless we wanted a higher profit margin)**
We would give a RRP for this skirt at **330.00**

One way in which we could reduce our total cost price would be to use less expensive linen fabric and lining and try to negotiate a better cmt price from our factory as my target RRP for this skirt could be **299**, which is a more sensible price point, so I would aim to wholesale this skirt for **107** approx (299 divided by 2.8) In the case of Style QA100 I would drop the overhead charge if I could not user a lesser fabric or re-negotiate my cmt price.

All costing sheets differ in appearance and in detail. Some costing sheets allow columns for adding in your profit margin so all is contained on one sheet.

Terms and Conditions UK and Republic Of Ireland

ORDER ACCEPTANCE

All new orders are subject to a credit check and required to provide trade and bank references.
Orders are only processed after satisfactory references.

TERMS AND PAYMENT

30 Days Net.
At all times retention of goods will remain the property of (Your name/company) until payment has been received in full and cleared. Interest will be charged on all outstanding monies including V.A.T on any account over 30 days. Interest will be charged at the current rate. All legal costs incurred in recovery of outstanding monies will be passed to the customer.

BANK DETAILS

(Insert you full bank details here)

DELIVERY

Ex-Warehouse within delivery dates specified unless alternative delivery has been approved. Any preference for separate carriage by carriers other than those approved by (Your name/company) will be at the customers own risk and any extra costs will be passed onto the customer. Carriage and or postal will be charged on all orders of less than one thousand pounds GBP.

SHORTAGE AND NON-DELIVERY

All shortage and non delivered goods must be notified to (Your name/company) within 2 working days of delivery. Responsibility for damaged or stolen items will be with the customer unless all reasonable effort has been made to both notify the carrier and (Your name/company). Whilst we make every effort to deliver all orders complete, we reserve the right to amend shipments where necessary.

RETURNS

(Your name/company) allows 7 days for customer inspection. After this period no returns will be accepted for any reason. Returns note must accompany all returns itemizing all returns in style, colour, and size and quoting invoice number. Credit notes will only be issued after the warehouse has signed off return notes and confirmed returns.

CANCELLATION

(Your name/company) only accept cancellations within 15 days after the original date of order. After that date cancellations will be charged at the following rate:

Days before delivery	Order cost
120 days	30%
90 days	60%
30 days	100%

JURISDICTION

Any contract of sale and supply of goods is made and the understanding that any dispute relating to said sale and supply of goods will be within the jurisdiction of English Courts and be covered by the law of England and Scotland
(Your name/company)

Trade Reference Form - Example

Re:

Dear Sir/Madam,

The above business has applied to open a credit account with us and have given your company details as a trade reference.

It would assist us greatly if we could ask you a number of short questions in this regard. We in turn would be happy to return any such information should we be approached to complete a trade reference from yourselves. Thank you in anticipation.

How long have you traded with the retailer?

What are your terms of payment?

What is there given credit limit?

Are their payments prompt/average/slow?

Does the account require excess supervision?

Payment by cheque/telegraphic transfer?

High/average or low returns rate?

Any other relevant information?

Be assured, we treat any information supplied in the strictest of confidence and we accept any information supplied attracts no liability on your part.
If you are able to fax the form to me directly on .... I would be extremely grateful.

Yours faithfully

Tips & Tricks Sheet

Make your mail out effective. It must stand out from all the others buyers receive

Small cards are a cost effective & proven strategy for sales campaigns.

Only use email campaigns in conjunction with a hard copy mail out. Never send unsolicited emails to buyers, it will go to their junk files

Target a reasonable amount of buyers to call. 40 - 50 are reasonable but send the mail out to every single buyer on the database.

Do not drive buyers mad with persistent phone calls! They really hate this
Your object is to make an appointment, preferably at their store initially.

Always confirm appointments. Buyers forget, double book & change their plans often! At this point try to get an email address for the buyer

Always allow & prompt buyers to try samples on but make sure you tell them it's a 1st sample and not a fit sample. Always have a floor standing mirror available.

Only Talk about minimum orders when prompted & then mention the minimum order to be approx 35 pieces. Do not talk payment terms until writing the order.

30 days net is standard. 2.5% discount for payment 7 days is standard. Terms & conditions must be signed.

Do not offer exclusivity unless the order reflects a good buy and represents the collection entirely. Even then try to steer away from complete exclusivity.

Quote a minimum exclusivity distance between stores of 15 - 20 miles radius.

Always have a line plan for buyers to take away. Look books are useful too but line plans contain price info, colour info & size info.

Try to obtain at least two trade references. Have a new account form printed out.

A Pro-forma payment means you make the goods, and then call for payment prior to shipping.

C.O.D means payment upon receipt of goods.

Try to accept a small deposit for the order but talk through with the buyer 1st. This may not be possible in today's retail climate but do not lose the order because of it. Negotiate.

Delivered Duty Paid (DDP) terms means that if you are shipping the goods to your customer using these terms, it is up to you to insure the goods and absorb all the costs and risks including payment and fees.

The above term (DDP) is a commonly used INCOTERM developed for international trade by The International Chamber of Commerce. The best website which outlines and explains all commonly used INCOTERMS such as FOB, CIF, EX-Works can be found at **www.foreign-trade.com**

Never offer Sale or Return terms unless it's firmly in your favour to do so.

Always ask buyers if they have found anything special this season - they love to brag!

Ask if they have dropped any labels this season. It will give you an insight into their current trading situation. Ask about their best performing labels.

Try not to appoint an agent, showroom or distributor in your first/second selling season. You will have more negotiating powers if you have a few stockists first.

No confident agent will ask for more than 15% commission payable to them on invoiced amounts no more than 7 days after the store has paid you.

Any distributor who requests more than 33.3% off your wholesale price must guarantee you an order in excess of 150 - $250,000 per season Remember, negotiate sensible, realistic terms.

When contemplating a distributorship deal always remember that the distributor themselves will be your sole customer, they receive a single bulk order from you. Once you deliver to their warehouse, they will individually pick & pack this shipment to supply each individual store they have sold to. They invoice & chase payment from these stores. You are not involved. It is your responsibility to ensure you are paid on time & in full for the bulk order you have supplied to the distributor. They are your customer.

The Top 400 + Men's & Women's Buyer & Retail Directory.

Womenswear Directory

Ms Tiffany Lewis 01730 265 466
Buyer
20 The High Street
Petersfield
Hampshire, UK GU32 3JL

Ms Josephine Turner 0207 730 7180
Buyer
A La Mode
10 Symons Street
London, UK SW3 2TJ

Ms Adele. 01920 463311
Buyer
Adele
Rankin House
High Street Ware
Herts, UK SG12 9EE

Mr Carl Jacklin 01522 543956
Owner/Buyer
Agatha
262a High Street
Lincoln LN2 1HW

E-mail:info@agatha-boutique.co.uk
www.agatha-boutique.co.uk

Ms Val Heng- Vong 0207 221 7070
Owner/Buyer
Aime 32-34 Ledbury Road
London W11 2AB

Mrs Odette Azagury 0207 935 6506
Owner/Buyer
Alberre Odette
14 Hinde Street
London W1U 3BF

Ms Gina Singleton 017 5861 2623
Buyer
Alcatraz
14-16 Gaol Street
Pwellheli
Gwynedd LL53 5RG

Mrs Carla Helmholz 001 503 224 1647
Owner/Buyer
Alder & Co
537 SW 12th Avenue
Portland
Oregon, USA 97205

Ms Susan Tier 01242 519452
Owner/Buyer
Alison Harrison
3 The Courtyard
Montpellier, Cheltenham
Gloucestershire GL50 1SR

Ms Michelle Lewis 0117 974 3882
Buyer
Allure
17 Regent Street
Clifton Village
Bristol BS8 4HW
E-mail: Michelle@allure-fashions.co.uk
www.allure-fashions.co.uk

Ms Alison Carter 01223 309 657
Buyer
Ally Lulu
40 Green Street
Cambridge
Cambs CB2 3JX

Amelia. 01548 844 445
Owner/Buyer
Amelias Attic
9 Fore Street
Salcombe
Devon TQ8 8BY

Ms Ann Day 01865 513266
 Buyer
Ann Day
31 Walton Street
Oxford
Oxon, UK OX2 6AA

Mrs Anna Park 0207 483 0411
Owner/ Buyer
126 Regent Park Road
Primrose Hill
London, UK NW1 8XL

Mrs Eleonora Browne 01225 447578
Owner/Buyer
Annabel Harrison
Unit 14/15 Shires Yard
Milsom Street
Bath BA1 1BZ

E-mail: eleonora@ah-moda.com

Mrs Shirley Wong 0208 6933342
Owner/Buyer
Aqua 2
79 Dulwich Village
Dulwich
London SE21 7BJ

Ms Jane 01625 425 139
Owner
Arabella
40 Chestergate
Macclesfield
Cheshire SK11 6BA

Mrs Ann Mead 01206 577 507
Owner/Buyer
Arana
15 Crouch Street
Colchester
Essex, UK CO3 3EN

Ms Elizabeth Richards 01432 378385
Buyer
Artisan
15 Church Street
Hereford, UK HR1 2LR

Ms Hayley Beech 0207 756 1000
Premium Wear Buyer
ASOS.Com
2nd Floor, Greater London House
Hampstead Road
London NW1 7FB

E-mail:Hayleyb@asos.com
Web site:afiraa@asos.com (assistant buyer)

Ms Natalie Wright 0207 756 1000
Accessories Buyer
ASOS.com
2nd Floor, Greater London House
Hampstead Road
London NW1 7FB

E-mail: Nataliew@asos.com

Ms Sarah Lyles
Owner/Buyer 01943 607607
Attic
9b Leeds Road
Ilkley
West Yorkshire LS29 8DH

E-mail: sarahlyles@mac.com

Mrs Auriol Rickwood-Dodsworth 0191 281 2817
Owner/Buyer
Aura
4 Clayton Road
Jesmond
Newcastle Upon Tyne NE2 4RP

Ms Kara Feeney 028 8772 9097
Owner/Buyer
Aurora
63 Scotch Street
Dungannon, Ireland BT70 1BD

E-mail: kara@auroraboutique.co.uk
www.auroraboutique.co.uk

Ms Katie Lopez
Owner/Buyer
Austique Limited 0207 376 3663
330 Kings Road
London, UK SW3 5UR

E-mail Address:Clemmie@austique.co.uk

Mr Mathew Murphy 0207 499 6628
Ladieswear Buyer
B Store
6 Conduit Street
London, UK W1S 2XE

Ms Dena Stemmer 0161 773 5554
Buyer/Owner
Bal Harbour
55 Bury Old Road
Prestwich
Manchester M25 OFG

Ms Suzanne Davenport 01625 502520
Womens Designerwear Buyer
Bank Fashions
Unit 8 Bridge Street Mills
Union street, Macclesfield
Cheshire, UK SK11 6QG

Ms Tina Ferguson 0207 486 7779
Partner/Buyer
Bare
8 Chiltern Street
London W1U 7PU

Ms Tracey Birkin 01482 644 605
Owner/Buyer
Beau Monde
2 The Weir
Hessle
Hull HU13 0RU

Ms Karen Tearle 0208 465 5777
Owner/Buyer
Belle
20 College Approach
Greenwich
London SE10 9HY

Ms Julia .01993 822315
Bellinda
65 High Street
Burford
Oxon OX18 4QA

Ms Louise Ingham 01335 342 982
Buyer
Bennetts
19 - 23 St John's Street
Ashbourne Derbyshire DE6 1GP

Mrs Helene/ Barry Rappaport 01372 464 604
Bernards
4 -6 High Street
Esher
Surrey, UK KT10 9RT

Ms Kate Bonhote 0207 437 7338
Creative Director
Beyond The Valley
2 Newburgh Street
Newburh Quarter Carnaby Street
London W1F 7RD

www.beyondthevalley.com

Ms Kristjana S. Williams 0207 437 7338
Creative Director
Beyond The Valley
2 Newburgh Street
Newburgh Quarter Carnaby Street
London W1F 7RD

www.beyondthevalley.com

Zoe/Jenny . 01872 261 750
Buyers
Bishop Phillpotts ladieswear
Quay street
Truro
Cornwall, UK TR1 2HE

Ms Laura Lever 0208 905 4644
Buyer
Blu
1 Canons Corner
Stanmore, Middlesex
London HA8 8AE

Ms Anna Fern 01625 583 107
Owner/Buyer
Blue Lagoon
46 London Road
Alderley Edge
Cheshire SK9 7DZ

Mrs Claire Moore 01245 250083
Owner
Blue Lawn
1 Canbridge Way
Chelmsford
Essex, UK CM2 OBX

Ms Joan Kershaw 01253 622 358
Owner/Buyer
Blueberries
101 - 103 Topping Street
Blackpool
Lancashire, UK FY1 3AA

Bod & Ted. 01892 526700
Owner/Buyers
Bod & Ted
The Old Post Office
Market Street, Salcombe
Devon TQ8 8DE
Web site:www.bodandted.co.uk

Lisa 029 2039 7025
Owner/Buyer
Body Basics
79 Pontcanna Street
Cardiff CF11 9HS

Jenny & Deb 0131 447 7701
Owner/Buyers
Bohemia
33a Morningside Road
Edinburgh EH9 1JH

Mrs Elizabeth Taylor 01706 231674
owner/Buyer
Bolthole
9 Alder Avenue
Rossendale
Lancs BB4 7RZ

Mrs Marilyn Mitchell 01442 865347
Owner
Boltons
153 High Street
Berkhampstead HP4 3HB

Ms Louise Kavanagh 0151 236 6001
Owner/Buyer
Boudoir Boutique
1 Cavern Walks
Liverpool L2 6RE

E-mail: sales@boudoir-boutique.com
www.boudoirboutique.com

Ms Pippa Sandison 01223 323000
Owner/Buyer
Boudoir Femme
18 King Street
Cambridge CB1 1LH

Ms Alexandra Esposito 00353 59 9139099
Owner/Buyer
Bourbon
19 Dublin Street
Carlow
Dublin, Ireland

Ms Karen Harries
Buyer 0208 981 7175
Boutiqueye
10 Albany Works
Gunmakers Lane
London E3 5PP

Ms Rosalind Bown 01223 302000
Owner/Buyer
Bowns CK
25 Magdalene Street
Cambridge
Cambs, UK CB3 OAS

Ms Bridget Salmassian 0208 946 7073
Owner
Bridget Salmassian
2 Church Road
Wimbledon Village
London, UK SW19 5DL

E-mail: bridget@salmassian.com

Ms Ellen Armstrong 01707 339333
Owner/Buyer
Brooks
39 Fretherne Road
Welwyn Garden City
Herts, UK AL8 6NS

E-mail: Ellen@brooksstyle.biz
www.brooksstyle.biz

Ms Ann Comerford 00353 1605 6666
Buyer - Ladies accesories
Brown Thomas
Cavendish House
Lemon Street
Dublin 2

E-mail: acomerford@brownthomas.ie

Ms Karen Higgins 00353 1605 6666
Contemporary Designerwear Buyer 00353 868229794
Brown Thomas
Cavendish House
Lemon Street
Ireland Dublin 2

E-mail: khiggins@brownthomas.ie

Ms Pamela Mooney 00353 1605 6666
Buyer - Ladies Cosmetics
Brown Thomas
Cavendish House
Lemon Street
Dublin 2

Ms Erin Mullaney 0207 514 0009
Senior Buyer
Browns
23-27 South Molton Street
London, UK W1Y 1DA

Ms Tiffany Start 0207 514 0071
Buyer
Browns Focus
38 - 39 South Molton Street
London W1K 5RN

E-mail: tiffany.start@brownsfashion.com

Ms Claire Heathcoate 01200 426 293
Owner/Buyer
Browse
42 King Street
Whalley, Clitheroe
Lancashire BB7 2EU

Mr Mark Donaldson 0033 442 969 254
Owner/Buyer
Buddha
29 Rue Boulegon 1310
Aix - en - Provence
France

Mrs Pam Fisher
Owner/Buyer
Cabana
26 Hatter Street
Bury St Edmonds
SuffolkIP33 1NE

Mr Alexander Edwards 01962 877399
Buyer
Cadogan
30 - 31 The Square
Winchester
Hampshire S023 9EX

Ms Rebecca Burgoyne 01179 738 040
Buyer
Cadogan Bristol Ltd
30 The Mall
Clifton, Avon
Bristol BS8 4DS

Ms Alison McMechan 01736 799880
Owner/Buyer
Calico
39a Fore Street
St Ives
Cornwall, UK TR26 1HE

Ms Lynne Beggs 02892 683273
Owner/Buyer
Candy Plum
4 Main Street
Hillsborough BT26 6AE

www.candyplum.co.uk

Ms Zara Beggs 02892 683 273
Owner/Buyer
Candy Plum
4 Main Street
Hillsborough BT26 6AE
www.candyplum.co.uk

Mr James Hurdis 01332 205 058
Buyer
Canopy
7 Sadler Gate
Derby
Derbyshire DE1 3NF

Mrs Carol Grant 01743 368182
Owner/ Buyer
Carol Grant
13 The Square
Shrewsbury
Shropshire SY1 1LH

Mrs Caroline Blair 01539 730500
Owner/Buyer
Caroline Blair
10 Library Road
Kendal, UK LA9 4QB

Janis/ Dave 01232 243 412
Buyers
Carter
45 Howard Street
Spires Mall
Belfast, Ireland BT1 6NE

Ms Chrissy Watson 01892 526 916
Buyer
Catwalk
26 High Street
Tunbridge Wells
Kent TN1 1DA

Chris. 0207 408 1596
Owner/Buyer
Changing Room
10a Gees Court
London, UK W1M 5HG

Ms Carol Florry 01892 547 899
Buyer
Changing Room
8 High Street
Tunbridge Wells
Kent TN1 1UX

Mrs Sam Cuthbert 01438 712 200
Buyer
Chanticleer
7 & 9 High Street
Welwyn
Herts AL6 9EE

Mrs Sangita Ebrahim 0208 883 9151
Owner/ Buyer
Charli
102 Muswell Hill Broadway
London, UK N10 3RS

E-mail: fashion@charli.co.uk
www.charli.co.uk

Ms Rebecca Cargill
Owner/Buyer
Chattertons
The Old Bank
55 High Street, Old Amersham
Bucks, UK HP7 0DR

Ms Danielle Palmer 029 2025 6140
Buyer
Chessmen
10 - 14 Castle Arcade
Cardiff CS10 1BU

Ms Dawn Hodgkinson 01823 663562
Owner/Buyer
Chica's
25 The Brambles
Wellington
Somerset TA21 9PS

E-mail: dawn.hodgkinson@tesco.net

Ms Yochi Davis 01708 742 231
Ladies Buyer
Choice Ltd
Unit 2 Spring Garden Industrial Estate
London Road, Romford
Essex RM7 9LD

Ms Kay Lennox 00 353 1 832 1130
Owner/Buyer
Clothespeg
Sutton Cross Shopping Centre
Sutton Cross
Dublin 13, Ireland

Ms Eftychia Georgilis 0207 435 9377
Owner/Buyer
Cochinechine
74 Heath Street
London NW3 1DN

Mrs Nicola Johnson 01704 513 393
Owner/Buyer
Coco Boutique
3-7 Wayfarers Arcade
Lord Street, Southport
Merseyside PR8 1NT

E-mail:cocoboutiquelive.co.uk

Ms Jennifer Burton 01872 225 887
Buyer
 Coco Marie
11 Kenwyn Street
Truro TR1 3OJ

Ms Alison Chow 0845 456 8880
Owner/Buyer
Coco Ribbon
21 Kensington Park Road
NottingHill
London W11

Ms Lisa Newman 01132 613 063
Buyer
Collections
141 The Avenue
Off Alwoodley Lane, Leeds
West Yorkshire LS17 7PA

Ms Nina Grant 0131 556 3707
Owner/Buyer
Corniche
2-4 Jeffrey Street
Edinburgh EH1 1DT

Ms Julia Jaconelli 01483 452825
Owner/Buyer
Courtyard
5-6 Angelgate
Guildford
Surrey, UK GU1 4AE
www.courtyard.co.uk

Ms Julie Heathcote 01273 609515
Buyer
Covet
16 Gloucester Road
Brighton
East Sussex BN1 4AD

Ms Pavla Henshaw 01392 211009
Owner/Buyer
Crede Boutique
Little Castle Street
Exeter
Devon EX4 3PX
E-mail:pavla@credeboutique.co.uk

Ms Justine Mills 0151 227 4645
Buyer
Cricket
10 Cavern Walk
Mathew Street, Liverpool
Merseyside, UK L2 6RE

Opi 01223 262123
Owner/Buyer
Cuckoo Clothing Limited
Burwash Manor, New Road, Barton
Cambridgeshire CB23 7AY

Ms Natasha Reilly 01563 852200
Womenswear Buyer
D2
Marathon House Olympic Business Centre
Day Bridge Road, Dundonald
Kilmarnock KA2 9AE

Mrs Heba Al – Okar 00974 5510287
Owner/Buyer
Dado's
P.O Box 23448
Dohar
Qatar
E-mail: habhoub15@hotmail.com

Mr Alan Kane
Owner/Buyer
Dais Boutique
2nd Floor Byram Arcade
Westgate
Huddersfield

Ms Cathy Smyth 028 3026 7113
Owner/Buyer
Dali
26 Bridge Street
Newry
County Down BT35 8AE
Web site www.daliboutique.co.uk

Kat & Aalam . 0208 987 8571
Owner/Buyers
Damsel
11a Devonshire Road
London W4 2EU

Ms Susan Turner 01723 379134
Buyer
Dapper Woman
30 St Nicholas Street
Scarborough YO11 2HF

Mr Dar 0207 240 7577
Owner/Buyer
Dar Dar
53 Monmouth Street
Covent Garden
London, UK WC2H 9DG

Debby Tachini 0030 6972 636334
Owner Buyer
De Toute Facon
Tsakalof 32
10673 Kolonaki
Athens, Greece

Ms Deborah Lenderyou 01273 473 367
Owner/Buyer
Delilah
90 High Street
Lewes
BN7 1XN

Satoshi Okitsu 0207 432 7610
Buyer
Design Works
Abahouse Uk Ltd
42-44 Broadwick Street, Soho
London W1F 7AE

Gillian Nicholson 0191 2815351
Buyer
Designer
15a Clayton Road
Jesmond
Newcstle Upon Tyne NE2 4RO

Kate Gaffney 003531 833 1592
Owner/ Buyer
Diffusion
47 Clontarf Road
Dublin 3
Eire, Ireland

E-mail Address:diffusion@eircom.net

Contacts
Kate Gaffney 003531 833 1592
Owner Buyer

Mr Carl Peddie 01902 716 762
Buyer
Diffusion Ltd
68 Victoria Street
Wolverhampton WV1 3NX

Ms Gabrielle Parker 0207 359 8877
Womenswear Buyer
Diverse
294 Upper Street
Islington
London, UK N1 2TZ

Ms Donna Ida 0207 225 3816
Owner/Buyer
Donna Ida
106 Draycott Avenue
London SW3 3AE

www.donnaida.com

Ms Dorothea Vernon 01926 334880
Buyer
Dorothea
16 Park Street
Leamington Spa
Warwickshire, UK CV32 4QN

Mrs Shirley Doyle 01858 433 279
Owner/ Buyer
Doyles Clothing
Old Town Hall, Church Street,
Market Harborough
Leicestershire, UK LE16 7AA

Ms Victoria Hawley 01858 462175
Buyer
Doyles Clothing
The Old Town Hall
Church Street, Market Harborough
Leicestershire LE16 7AA

Ms Vixy Rae 0141 552 5451
Buyer
Dr Jives
111 - 113 Candleriggs
Glasgow G1 1NP

Ms Deidre Fenton 003+5 (387) 275-0641
Owner/Buyer
Dress
27 Pearse Street
Athlone
Co Westmeath, Ireland

Ms Rebecca Skinner 01392 274 840
Director
Dukes Fine Clothes Ltd
Harlequins, Paul Street
 Exeter
Devon, UK EX4 3TT

Ms Elaine Curtis 00353 59 914 1790
Owner/Buyer
Elaine Curtis
122 Tullow Street
Carlow, Ireland

Ms Linda Leversuch 01325 281 816
Buyer
Elan
Unit 3 Grange Road
Darlington
County Durham DL1 5NH

Ms Nickey Thrussell 0207 449 0574
Owner/Buyer
Elias and Grace
158 Regents Park Road
Primrose Hill
London NW1 8XN
E-mail: Info@eliasandgrace.com
www.eliasandgrace.com

Ms Elizabeth Charles +1 212 243 3201
Owner/Buyer
Elizabeth Charles
639 1/2 Hudson Street
New York NY
10014, USA

Ms Elizabeth Charles +1 415 440 2100
Owner/Buyer
Elizabeth Charles
2056 Fillmore Street
San Francisco
CA, USA 94115

Ms Charlotte Rutter 0207 450 1459
Owner/Buyer
Ellie & Charlotte
117 St Johns Hill
Battersea
London SW11 1SZ
E-mail: info@ellieandcharlotte.com

Mrs Erin Welker 01590 677 818
Buyer
Elliots Ltd
44-46 High Street
Lymington
Hampshire SO4 19YS

Ms Susan Debae 01753 853 777
Ladies Buyer
Emilia
33 St Leonards Road
Windsor
Berkshire SL4 3BP

Ms Emma 003531 6339781
Owner/Buyer
Emma
33 Clarendon Street
Dublin 2, Ireland

E-mail: barnettemma@yahoo.com

Ms Deidre Docherty 028 906 63132
Owner/Buyer
Emporio
2 Lislea Avenue
Lisburn Road, County Down
Belfast BT9 7HQ

Ms Paula Jauncey 01905 726643
Owner/Buyer
Emporio
33 Friar Street
Worcester, UK WR1 2NA

Ms Joanne Maloney 0114 2701812
Buyer
Eton
14-16 Division Street
Sheffield S1 4GF

E-mail: etonclothing@btconnect.com

Ms Annette Oliviery 0207 243 1808
Buyer
Euforia
61b Lancaster Road
London, UK W11 1QG

Fall Woman 01565 754 488
35 King Street
Knutsford
Cheshire WA16 6DW

E-mail Address:info@fallwoman.com
www.fallwoman.com

Mrs Suzanne Burstein 0207 243 8800
Owner/Buyer
Feathers
176 Westbourne Grove
Notting Hill
London W11 2RW

Ms Diana Desloubibres 0207 629 9161
Assistant Buyer Womens International
Fenwick Limited
63 New Bond Street
London W1A 3BS

Ms Natasha Blacker 0207 629 9161
Buyer - Beauty Products
Fenwick Ltd
63 New Bond Street
London W1A 3BS

Ms Michelle Hughes 01892 516 716
Designer ladieswear Buyer
Fenwick Ltd
101 Royal Victoria Place
Tunbridge Wells
Kent TN1 2SR

Mrs Nicky Marks 0208 202 8200
Buyer - Ladies Accessories
Fenwick Ltd
Brent Cross Shopping Centre
Hendon
London NW4 3FN

Ms Sophia Powell 0207 629 9161
Buyer - Ladies accessories
Fenwick Ltd
63 New Bond Street
London W1A 3BS

Ms Karen Wilkinson 0208 202 8200
Buyer - Toiletries
Fenwick Ltd
Brent Cross Shopping Centre
Hendon
London NW4 3FN

E-mail: karen.wilkinson@fenwick.co.uk

Ms Catherine Gaskin 01227 766866
Ladies Designerwear Buyer
Fenwicks Limited
St Georges Street
Canterbury
Kent, UK CT1 2TB

Ms Ann Henderson 0208 202 8200
Ladies Designerwear Buyer
Fenwicks Limited
Brent cross Shopping Centre
Hendon
London, UK NW4 3FN

Ms Catherine Newton 0191 232 5100
Ladies designerwear Buyer
Fenwicks Limited
39 Northumberland Street
Newcastle Upon Tyne
UK NE99 1AR

Ms Emma Rochester 0207 629 9161
Womenswear International buyer
Fenwicks Limited
63 New Bond Street
London, UK W1A 3BS
E-mail: bondstreet.intbuying@fenwick.co.uk

Ms Jila Turner 0207 629 9161
Lingerie Buyer
Fenwicks Limited
63 New Bond Street
London W1A 3BS

Ms Georgina Coulter 0208 202 8200
Buyer, Boutique
Fenwicks Ltd
Brent Cross Shopping Centre
Hendon
London, UK NW4 3FN

Ms Fi Lovett 0207 352 3232
Buyer
FiFi Wilson
Chelsea Green
1 Godfrey Street
London SW3 3TA

www.fifiwilson.com

Ms Laura Poole 01580 762536
Owner/Buyer
Figis
11 Sayers Lane
Tenterden
Kent TN 30 6BW
E-mail: info@figisboutique.com

Ms Andy Lisle 02380 232 559
Buyer
Five - O -Store
16 East Bargate
Southampton
Hampshire S014 2DJ

Ms Heidi Smith 012 7347 4166
Buyer
Flint
70 High Street
Lewes
East Sussex BN7 1XG

Ms Jessica Britten 01491 412 323
Buyer
Fluidity
43 Bell Street, Nettlebed
Henley Upon Thames, Oxon
Oxfordshire RG9 2BA

Ms Suzie Harvie – Clarke 01491 412 323
Owner / Buyer
Fluidity
43 Bell street, Nettlebed,
Henley Upon Thames, Oxon
Oxfordshire, UK RG9 2BA

E-mail: Suziehc@hotmail.com

Mrs Dianne Yarlett 0208 295 1065
Buyer
Fortuny
22- 24 High Street
Chislehurst
Kent BR7 5AN

Ms Gemma Wiseman 01451 832 453
Owner/Buyer
Foundation
The Market Square
Stow- On-The-Wold
Gloucestershire, UK GL54 1AB

E-mail: jemma@shopfoundation.com
www.shopfoundation.com

Ms Marietta Fox 0207 228 4077
Owner/Buyer
Galleria Conti
22 Battersea Rise
London SW11 1EE

E-mail: george@continista.com
www.continista.com

Ms Helen Emerson 01273 692 691
Buyer
Garden
39b Sydney Street
The North Laine, Brighton
East Sussex BN1 4EP

Ms Lisa/steve Pomeranc 0208 458 9616
Buyer/Owner
Highhaven limited
London, UK NW11 7BD
Contacts
Lisa Pomeranc 0208 455 8909
Owner/Buyer

Ms Gill Holland 0208 299 6761
Owner/Buyer
Gill Holland
33 Dulwich Village
Dulwich SE21 7BN

Mrs Vivian Kingsley 01603 763 158
Owner/Buyer
Ginger
35 Timberhill
Norwich
Norfolk, UK NR1 3LA

Giulio Cinque 01223 316 100
Buyer
Giulio
46 King Street
Cambridge
Cambridgeshire, UK CB4 1VZ

Ms Alexa Kiourtzidis 0207 351 9314
Buyer
Gloss Lifestyle
159 Kings Road
London SW3 5TX

Ms Georgina Wright 01603 492021
Buyer
GMW Designs
Oasis Health Club
Pond Lane Thorpe St Andrew
Norwich, UK NR7 0UB

Ms Sara Thomas 01273 202366
Buyer ladies designerwear
Gog Shop
24 East Street
Brighton
East Sussex, UK BN1 1HL

Ms Alison Denton 01472 602738
Buyer
Guru
14 Seaview Street
Cleethorpes
Humberside DN35 8E2

Ms Hayley Meller 0207 586 4121
Buyer
Hanna Lee
77 St Johns Wood High Street
London, UK NW8 7SH

Mr Robert Crabtree 01422 353038
Owner/Buyer
Harold Crabtree
10 Market Street
Halifax
West Yorkshire HX1 1RN

Ms Carol Soloman 0207 722 9260
Owner/ Buyers
Harpers
84 St Johns Wood High Street
London NW8 7SH

Pippa Donovan 01702 585859
Owner/Buyer
Harpur & Co.
146 The Broadway
Thorpe Bay
Essex SS1 3ES

Ms Natalie Dangerfield
Lingerie Buyer
Harrods Ltd
87-135 Brompton Road
Knightsbridge
London SW1X 7XL
E-mail Address:Natalie.dangerfield@harrods.com

Ms Rebecca Dobbin 0207 730 1234
Buyer-Luxury Collections & Modern Classics
Harrods Ltd
87-135 Brompton Road
Knightsbridge
London SW1X 7XL

E-mail Address:rebecca.dobbin@harrods.com

Ms Anna Foreman 0207 893 8062
Assistant Buyer for Scarves
Harrods Ltd
87-135 Brompton Road
London SW1X 7XL

E-mail Address:anna.foreman@harrods.com

Ms Torly Grimshawe 0207 730 1234
Concession Manager ladies fashion/beauty
Harrods Ltd
87-135 Brompton Road
Knightsbridge
London, UK SW1X 7XL

E-mail Address:Torly.Grimshawe@harrods.com

Ms Kerry Jones 0207 893 8269
Buyer - Way In Dept
Harrods Ltd
Way In
87-135 Brompton Road
Knightsbridge
London, UK SW1X 7XL

E-mail Address:Kerry.jones@harrods.com
Web site:Vanina.balseiro@harrods.com

Mr Philip Jones 0207 730 1234
Designer Studio buyer
Harrods Ltd
87-135 Brompton Road
Knightsbridge
London, UK SW1X 7XL
E-mail Address:Philip.jones@harrods.com

Ms Sophie Kerr 0207 893 8704
Senior Clerk For Soft Accessories
Harrods Ltd
87-135 Brompton Road
London SW1X 7XL

E-mail Address:sophie.kerr@harrods.com
Ms Sue Shields 0207 730 1234
Buyer of Soft Accessories
Harrods Ltd
87-135 Brompton Road
Knightsbridge
London SW1X 7XL

E-mail Address:sue.shields@harrods.com
Mrs Maria Harvey 01780 755850

Owner/Buyer
Harvey
7 Iron Monger Street
Stamford
Lincolnshire, UK PE9 1PL

Ms Shareen Basma
International Buyer
Harvey Nichols
67 Brompton Road
Knightsbridge
London SW3 1DB
E-mail: shareen.basma@harveynichols.com

Ms Coco Chan 0207 235 5000
Contemporary Designerwear
Harvey Nichols
67 Brompton Road
Knightsbridge
London, UK SW3 1DB

Ms Deidre Cullen 0207 201 8609
Buying Administrator- Designer Collections
Harvey Nichols
67 Brompton Road
LondonSW3 1DB
E-mail: Deirdre.Cullen@harveynichols.com

Ms Charlotte Greenhalgh 0207 235 5000
Lingerie/Swimwear Buyer
Harvey Nichols
67 Brompton Road
Knightsbridge
London SW3 1DB

Ms Victoria Hill 0207 201 8568
Assistant Buyer - Contemporary Accessories
Harvey Nichols
67 Brompton Road
Knightsbridge
London SW3 1DB

E-mail Address:victoria.hill@harveynichols.com

l Vikki Kavanagh 0207 235 5000
Buyer - Leisurewear
Harvey Nichols
67 Brompton Road
Knightsbridge
London SW3 1DB

E-mail Address:Vikki.Kavanagh@harveynichols.com

Ms Tina Lamb 0207 235 5000
Senior Buyer- Women's Accessories
Harvey Nichols
67 Brompton Road
Knightsbridge
London SW3 1DB
E-mail Address:tina.lamb@harveynichols.com

Ms Averyl Oates 0207 201 8514
Buying Director
Harvey Nichols
67 Brompton Road
Knightsbridge
London SW3 1DB

E-mail: Averyl.Oates@harveynichols.com
Web site:april.glassborow@harveynichols.com

Ms Ida Peterson 0207 235 5000
Assistant Buyer Ladies Accessories
Harvey Nichols
67 Brompton Road
Knightsbridge
London SW3 1DB

Ms Daniella Rinaldi
Head of perfumery
Harvey Nichols
67 Brompton Road
Knightsbridge
London SW3 1DB

Ms Helena Sotiriou 0207 235 5000
Buyer - Ladies Gloves
Harvey Nichols
67 Brompton Road
Knightsbridge
London SW3 1DB

E-mail Address:helena.sotiriou@harveynichols.com

Ms Helena Sotiriou 0207 235 5000
Assistant Buyer Ladies Accessories
Harvey Nichols
67 Brompton Road
Knightsbridge
London SW3 1DB

Ms Charlotte Southern 0207 235 5000
Buyer - Designer Collections
Harvey Nichols
67 Brompton Road
Knightsbridge
Londo SW3 1DB

E-mail:Charlotte.Southern@harveynichols.com
Web site:deirdre.cullen@harveynichols.com

Ms Nicky Creedon 00 353 1 260 2707
Buyer
Havana
68 Donnybrrok Road
Dublin, Ireland Dublin 4

Ms Kate Walton 0191 213 1155
Owner/Buyer
Have to Love
1-3 Hawthorn Road
Gosforth
Newcastle Upon Tyne NE3 4DE

www.havetolove.com

Ms Sarah Bell 0207 896 7539
Buyer
Heal & Son Ltd
196 Tottenham Court Road
London W1T 7LQ

Ms Liza Gale 0208 441 3232
Owner/Buyer
Heaven on the Green
203 High Street
Hadley Green
Herts, UK EN5 5SU

Ms Emma Taylor 0207 259 9426
Buyer
Heidi Klein
257 Pavillion Road
London SW1X OBP

E-mail Address:emma@heidiklein.co.uk

Lesley Delamare 01223 328 740
Buyer
Hero
3 Green Street
Cambridge
 Cambs, UK CB2 3JU

Mrs Rama Shalin +2 (012) 210-8126
Owner/Buyer
Hip
48 Giza Street
Cairo, Egypt
E-mail: Ramashalin@tedata.net.eg

Ms Annie Brocklebank 01722 411 051
Owner/Buyer
Hollyhock
25-27 New Street
Salisbury
Wiltshire SP1 2PH

Ms Avril Newcombe 01242 527505
Fashion Buyer Womenswear
Hoopers
The Promenade
Cheltenham
Glouc., UK GL7 2Q7

Ms Claudia Battistel 0207 003 4000
Branded Colections/Accessories
House Of Fraser
27 Baker Street
London W1U 8AH

Ms Sasha Buckley 0207 003 4320
Retail & Branding Manager
House Of Fraser
27 Baker Street
London W1U 8AH

E-mail Address:sbuckley@hof.co.uk

Ms Stephanie Chen 0207 003 4000
Director Of Womenswear
House Of Fraser
27 Baker Street
London W1U 8AH

Ms Sue Dunn 0207 003 4000
Head Of Concessions
House Of Fraser
27 Baker Street
London W1U 8AH

Ms Amanda Lepar 0207 003 4000
Lingerie Buyer
House Of Fraser
27 Baker Street
London W1U 8AH

Ms Rebbecca Morris 0207 003 4000
Young Fashion Buyer
House Of Fraser
27 Baker Street
London W1U 8AH

Ms Lee Prosser 0207 003 4000
Swim, Sunshine & Sleepwear Buyer
House Of Fraser
27 Baker Street
London W1U 8AH

Ms Nicola Sugden 0208 828 1000
Senior Buyer -Accessories
House Of Fraser
171 Victoria Street
London SW1E 5NN

E-mail Address:nsugden@hof.co.uk
Web site:abruton@hof.co.uk (Buyer)

Ms Louise Harries 0207 684 2083
Buyer
Hoxton Boutique
2 Hoxton Street
London, UK N1 6NG

Ms Gee 0207 485 1864
Buyer
Hutton
22 Chalk Farm Road
London NW1 8AG

Ms Zoe Ellison 01273 734 160
Buyer
i GiGi
37 Western Road
Hove
East Sussex BN3 1AF

Mrs Maria Vilela 0207 580 6434
Merchandiser
Iberica Trading
41/42 Eastcastle Street
London, UK W1W 8DU

Ms Lorna Mosely 0208 559 1540
Buyer
Icon
52 Queens Road
Buckhurst Hill
Essex IG9 5BY

Ms Maggie Howie 01224 646 380
Owner/Buyer
Image
42 Thistle Street
Aberdeen
Aberdeenshire AB1 OXD

Min Stevenson 01225 312115
Director
Image
9 Shires Yard
Milsom Street
Bath BA1 1BZ

Ms Julie Harrison
Owner/Buyer
Image Fashion Boutique
c/o Lovelace House
Wissenden Lane, Bethersden
Kent TN26 3AJ

Ms Heidi DeVries 01243 789 099
Buyer
Indigo
2 Baffins Court
Baffins Lane, Chichester
West Sussex PO19 1UA

Ms Anne Pollet 0207 372 1777
Owner/Buyer
Iris
73 Salusbury Road
London NW6 6NJ
Ms Irena Vajagic 0207 636 7130
Sales & Marketing manager
James Lakeland
12 Ogle Street
London 1W 6HU

E-mail Address: irena@jameslakeland.net

Ms Sarah Davidson 0131 225 3280
Owner/ Buyer
Jane Davidson
52 Thistle Street
Edinburgh
Midlothian EH2 1EN
E-mail Address: shop@janedavidson.co.uk

Ms Jane Kingsly 01636 703511
Owner/Buyer
Jane Young
Chain Lane
Market Place, Newark
Notts, UK NG24 1AU

www.janeyoung.co.uk

Ms Sarah Petitt 01488 682 472
Owner/Buyer
Jeanne Petitt
3 Bridge Street
Hungerford
Berkshire, UK RG17 OEH
E-mail Address: jeannepetitt@btconnect.com

Ms Elizabeth Hunter 0131 260 2433
Buyer
Jenners
48 Princes Street
Edinburgh, Scotland EH2 2YJ

Ms Marianne Lindsay 0131 260 2433
Buyer
Jenners
48 Princes Street
Edinburgh, Scotland EH2 2YJ

Ms Laura Mayer 0208 458 7454
Owner/ Buyer
Jessimara
1115 Finchley Road
Temple Fortune
London, UK NW11 OQD

Ms Joanna Berryman 0207 935 7109
Owner/Buyer
Jezebell
59 Blandford Street
Marylebone
London   W1U 7HP

Ms Kate Brindley 0207 935 7109
Owner/Buyer
Jezebell
59 Blandford Street
Marylebone
London W1U 7HP

Ms Cathy Taylor 01217 118711
Owner/Buyer
Jilly Franka
14 Drury Lane
Solihull
West Midlands, UK B91 3BG

Ms Donna Carol 0207 828 1000
Buyer - Private Label
John Lewis
171 Victoria Street
London SW1E 5NN

Ms Fiona Caulfield 0207 828 1000
Buyer - Beauty self selection
John Lewis
171 Victoria Street
London SW1E 5NN

E-mail Address: fiona_caulfield@johnlewis.co.uk

Ms Jo Hamilton 0208 828 1000
Ladies Bags Buyer
John Lewis
171 Victoria Street
London SW1E 5NN

Ms Catherine Hardy 0207 592 5785
Central Buyer Branded Collections
John Lewis
171 Victoria Street
London, UK SWIE 5NN

Ms Nicola Hattersley 0208 828 1000
Buyer - Fashion Accessories
John Lewis
171 Victoria Street
London SW1E 5NN

E-mail Address: nicola_hattersley@johnlewis.co.uk

Ms Jo Hooper 0207 828 1000
Head of Womenswear
John Lewis
171 Victoria Street
London SW1 5NN

Ms Judy Graham 01242 517 726
Owner/ Buyer
Judy Graham
21 The Promenade
Cheltenham
Gloucestershire, UK GL50 1LE

Mrs Rhona Blades 0191 281 7855
Owner/ Buyer
Jules B
91-93 Osbourne Road
Newcastle Upon Tyne
Tyne & Wear NE2 2AN

Ms Debbie Potts 0207 229 8874
Owner/Buyer
JW Beeton
48-50 Ledbury Road
London W11

Ms Karin Cameron 01224 625 711
Buyer
Kafka
41 Union Terrace
Aberdeen
Aberdeenshire AB1 1NP

Ms Kate, Louise 00 353 45896222
Owner/ Buyers
Kalu
16 South Main Street
Naas
Co. Kildare, Ireland

E-mail Address:emporiumkalu@eircom.net

Ms Pam & Kay Cartwright 0121 704 2233
Owner/Buyers
Katherine Draisy
58 Drury Lane
Solihull
West Midlands B91 3BH

Ms Jeryn Macay 00 353 1 278 1646
Buyer
Khan
1 Rock Hill
Blackrock
Co Dublin, Ireland

Jane & Kate 0207 486 7855
Buyer
KJ's Laundry
74 Marylebone Lane
Marylebone
London W1U 2PU
E-mail Address:kate@kjslaundry.com

Ms Nicky King 0116 270 9190
Owner/ Buyer
Knightsbridge
5 Francis Street
Stoneygat
Leicester, UK LE2 2BE

Mr Paul Sexton 0207 240 4280
Owner/Buyer
Koh Samui
65-67 Monmouth Street
Covent Garden
LondonWC2

Ms Sasha Bezovski 0207 434 1316
Owner/Buyer
Kokontozai
57 Greek Street
Soho
London, UK W1D 3DX

Ms Justine Josephs 0207 434 1316
Store Manager
Kokontozai
57 Greek Street
London W1D 3DX

Ms Marjan Pejoski 0207 434 1316
Owner/Buyer
Kokontozai
57 Greek Street
London W1D 3DX

Ms Angela Burt 01253 500 855
Owner/ Buyer
Koo
111 Redbank Road
Bispham, Blackpool
Lancs, UK FY2 9HZ

Ms Linda Jerrum 01202 780033
Buyer
L'Amica
14 Post Office Road
Bournemouth
Dorset, UK BH1 1BA

Ms Francesca Forcolini 0207 354 9333
Buyer/Owner
Labour Of Love
193 Upper Street
Islington
London, UK N1 1RQ

Mrs D.A Rosser 01865 552094
Owner
Lacys
29 Little Clarendon Street
Oxford, UK OX1 2HU

Ms Alex Hobden 01628 477077
Owner/Buyer
Landmark
7-9 West Street
Marlow
Bucks SL7 2LS

E-mail Address:alex@landmarkclothing.co.uk

Ms Regine Saunders 0207 586 4530
Owner/Buyer
Larizia
78 St John's Wood High Street
London, UK NW3 6TE

Ms Nathalie Constanty 0207 602 0445
Consultant
Le Bon Marche
18 Irving Road
London W14 OJS
E-mail Address:constanty@btinternet.com

Leila London 0207 288 2992
Nadia Mounti
Owner/Buyer 204 Upper Street
Islington
London N1 1RQ
E-mail:www.leilalondon.com

Ms Sandy Bontout 0033 142 769 361
Owner/Buyer
Les Belles Images
74 rue Charlot
75003
Paris, France

Margaret/Mary. 00 353 91 564 540
Owners
Les Jumelles
11 Upper Abigate Street
Galway
Ireland

Ms Jane Davis
0207 734 1234
Womens Buying Director
Liberty PLC
210-220 Regent Street
London W1B 5AH

Ms Eleanor Robinson
0207 573 9841
Womenswear Buyer
Liberty PLC
210-220 Regent Street
London, UK W1B 5AH
E-mail Address:erobinson@liberty.co.uk

Ms Alexandra Stylianidif
Head of Womenswear & Accessories
Liberty Plc
210 - 220 Regent Street
London W1B 5AH
E-mail Address: astylianidif@liberty.co.uk

Ms Claire Allen 01488 684020
Owner/Buyer
Lielow
25 Charnham Street
Hungerford
Berkshire RG17 OEJ

Ms Sheila Gammie 01888 562 021
Buyer
Lifestyle
55 High Street
Turriff
Aberdeenshire AB5 7YH

Ms Victoria Lloyd 0207 801 9600
Buyer
Lilli diva
32 Lavender Hill
London SW11 5RL

Mrs Harmeet Basra 0207 247 4719
Owner/Buyer
Lilly Bling
11 Whitechapel Road
London E1 1DU

Ms Claire Threapleton 01423 502444
Buyer
Lily & Beau
23 Parliament Street
Harrogate
HG1 2QU

E-mail Address: claire@lilyandbeau.com

Mr Piero Ferraro 0207 794 1775
Buyer
Linea
8 Heath Street
Hampstead
London, UK NW3 6TE

Mrs Lynne Edwards 01243 533992
Owner/Buyer
Little London Holdings Ltd
Head Office
40 Little London
Chichester PO19 1PL

Ms Sue/Guy Ashworth 01423 521 404
Buyer/Owner
Lynx
20 West Park
Harrogate
North Yorkshire, UK HG1 1BJ

Ms Madelaine Leddington   0121 704 9454
Owner/ Buyer
Madelaine Ann
45 Drury Lane
West Midlands B91 3BP

Ms Sarah Farrar 01803 292198
Buyer
Maggie & Co
7a The Strand
Torquay
Devon, UK TQ1 2AA

Ms Maggie Blyth 0146 3783017
Owner/Buyer
Maggie Blyth
50 High Street
Beauly, Highland
Inverness IV4 7BX
E-mail Address:maggieblth@btconnect.com
www.maggieblyth.co.uk

Ms Elizabeth Bennett 028 9068 7775
Owner/Buyer
Mary and Martha
545 Lisburn Road
Belfast BT97 G9

Ms Bridget Cosgrave 0208 944 7820
Fashion Director
Matches
15a Welmar Mews
154 Clapham Park Road
London, UK SW4 7DD

Ms Lianne Wiggins 0208 944 7820
International Womenswear Buyer
Matches
15a Welmar Mews
154 Clapham Park Road
London, UK SW4 7DD

E-mai: lianne@matches.co.uk

Anna/Lalita .
Owner/Buyer
Me & Mya
Office
No.66 Chipstead Street
Fulham
London SW6 3SS

Mrs Lalita Russell - Smith
Owner/Buyer 01730 814476
Me & Mya
No 1 Knockhundred Row
Midhurst
West Sussex GU29 9DQ

Ms Emma . 01225 442250
Owner/Buyer
Mee
9a Bartlett Street
Bath BA1 2QZ

E-mail: mee@meemee.co.uk

Ms Michelle O'Doherty 00 44 28 902 333 03
Owner/Buyer
Michelle O'Doherty
7 - 9 Chichester Street
Belfast, N.Ireland BT1 4JA
E-mai:info@michelledoherty.com

Ms Linda Weale 0044 28 902 33303
Owner/Buyer
Michelle O'Doherty
7 - 9 Chichester Street
Belfast, N. Ireland BT1 4JA
E-mail:info@michelledoherty.com

Ms Rebekah Hay-Brown 0207 351 7192
Buying Office
Mimi
The Courtyard
250 King's Road
London, UK SW3 5UE

E-mail: rebekah@mimilondon.co.uk
www.mimilondon.co.uk

Jane Stock 01202 887 600
Buyer
Mine
2 East Street
Wimborne
Dorset BH21 1DS

Ms Mo Griffin 01785 850868
Owner/Buyer
Moet
41-43 High Street
Eccleshall
Staffs ST21 6BW
E-mail: sales@moetofeccleshall.co.uk

Mr & Mrs Martin / Sue Allard 01423 565 709
Owners/ Buyers
Morgan Clare
3 Montpellier Gardens
Harrogate
North Yorkshire, UK HG1 2TF
E-mail: katie@morganclare.co.uk

Ms Susan Nichols 01789 295 820
Buyer
Mosaique
10 Wood Street
Stratford Upon Avon
Warwickshire, UK CV37 6JE

Ms Joy Even-Cook 0207 937 6282
Owner/Buyer
Musa
31 Holland Street
London, UK W8 4NA

Ms Laura . 00353 518 54448
Owner/Buyer
Muse
92 The Quay
Waterford
Ireland
E-mail: ellisl@eircom.net
Web site: cloray@hotmail.com

Ms Zoe Lem 0207 841 7131
Owner/Buyer
My Sugarland
402-404 St John's Street
London EC1V 4NJ

www.mysugarland.co.uk

Ms Joanne Watkinson 0845 260 3880
Womenswear Buyer
My- Wardrobe
32-34 Lenton Lane
Nottingham NG7 2NR

Email: joanne@my-wardrobe.com

Contacts
Nikki Wright 0845 260 3880

Ms Najah Mohamed 0207 221 9797
Buyer
Nancy Pop
19 Kensington Park Road
London W11 2EU
Contacts
Helen Roysdotter
Owner/Buyer

Ms kirsty Murton 0800 044 5700
Womenswear Buyer
Net-a-Porter Ltd
1 the Village Offices
Westfield London, Ariel Way
London, UK WG12 7GF
E-mail Address: designers@net-a-porter.com

Ms Susan Warren 01797 227175
Owner/Buyer
Niche
17 East Street
Rye
East Sussex TN31 7JY
E-mail Address: sue@niche17.com

Ms Zara Jones 01244 322812
Buyer
Nichols & Co
5 Bridge Street Row
Chester CH1 1NW

Ms Jean Myles 01244 322 812
Buyer
Nichols & Co
5 Bridge Street Row
Chester CH1 1NW

Ms Kathy Erasmus 0207 584 2451
Owner/Buyer
Night Owls
50 Fulham Road
London SW3 6HH

Ms Annette Pettifer 01822 618 188
Buyer
No. 13
13 Duke Street
Tavistock
Devon PL19 OBA

Ms Norma . 0113 242 0569
Owner/Buyer
No.15
Thorntons Arcade
Leeds LS1 6LQ
E-mail: norma@no-15.co.uk

Ms Helen Maylin Broyd 01787 474 152
Buyer
No.19
19 High Street
Halstead
Essex CO9 2AA

Ms Rhonda . 01273 911006
Owner/Buyer
Nola
42 Gardner Street
Brighton BN1 1UN
 www.nolaboutique.co.uk

Onda . 01326 270456
Owner/Buyer
Onda
St Mawes
Cornwall TR2 5DQ
E-mail: shop@ondarocks.co.uk

Poppy . 01872 223149
Owner/Buyer
Opium
6 Nalders Court
Truro
Cornwall TR1 2XH

Ms Jill Townley 01254 395703
Owner/Buyer
Originals
368 Blackburn Road
West End ,OswaldTwistle
Lancs, UK BB5 4LZ

Ms Claire Hourigan 0161 839 7575
Owner/Buyer
Oyster
1 Booth Street
Pall Mall
Manchester M2 4DU

Ms Marie-claire Roper 02920 512331
Owner/Buyer
Papillon Rose Ltd
17 Elm Grove Road
Dinas Powys
Glamorgan CF64 4AA

Ms Tina Harris 0191 284 0405
Owner/Buyer
Partners
63 - 65 High Street
Gosforth
Newcastle Upon Tyne, UK NE3 4AA

Ms Louise Tiller 0161 832 8595
Buyer
Pastiche
7 & 9 Old Bank Street
Manchester M1 7PE

Ms Claire Corrigan n01534 769333
Owner/Buyer
Pebble Boutique
5 Market Street
St Helier
Jersey JE2 4WY
E-mail: boutique@ilovepebble.com
www.ilovepebble.com

Ms Tracy Glanville 01277 262062
Buyer
Pellini Moda
73 Hatton Road
Shenfield
Essex, UK CM15 8JD

Ms Mahyar . 01932 829 229
Owner/Buyer
Piajeh
12 Baker Street
Weybridge
Surrey KT13 8AU

Ms Marie . 0208 547 2762
Buyer
Pie Woman
Unit G25 The Bentalls Centre
Wood Street Entrance
Kingston Upon Thames, UK KT1 1TR

Ms Patricia Swadling 01708 742248
Owner/Buyer
Pierrot
81 Main Road
Gidea Park, Romford
Essex RM2 5EL

Ms Ellie Batty 0116 262 5535
Womenswear Buyer
Pilot
36-38 Silver Street
Leicester, UK LE1 5ET

Bhavna 0207 266 2365
Owner/Buyer
Pipa
1 Formosa Street
London W9 1EE

Ms Gemma Louise-Fox
Owner/Buyer 01628 521465
Plume
1 Lower Ventnor Cottage
Cookham
Berks SL6 9AU

Ms Carolyn Hall 0208 995 1717
Owner/Buyer
Polomo
5 Chiswick Common Road
London W4 1RR
E-mail Address: Carolyn@polomo.com

Ms Alexandra Braithwaite 0207 627 2020
Buyer
Pour Mia
809 Wandsworth Road
Battersea
London SW8 3JH

Ms Kate Evans 0207 377 6668
Buyer
Precious
16 Artillery Passage
Spitalfields
London E1 7LJ

Ms Geraldine Sanglier 01225 329933
Owner/Buyer
Prey Limited
3 York Buildings
George Street
Bath, UK BA1 2EB
E-mail Address:john@prey.co.uk

Mrs Jane Stanley 01271 324977
Owner/ Buyer
Private Collection 2
4 Holland Walk
Barnstaple
Devon, . EX31 1DW

Ms Julie Jackson 01670 503737
Buyer
Privilege
New Market
Morpeth
Northumberland, UK NE61 1PS

Ms Lily Ajoundanpour 01273 323 275
Buyer
Profile
25 Dukes Lane
Brighton
East Sussex, UK BN1 1BG

Ms Kerry Walker 01642 888333
Ladieswear Buyer
Psyche
175-187 Linthorpe Road
Middlesborough
Cleveland, UK TS1 4AU

Ms Nicky Harper 01273 604 861
Buyer
Pussy
3a Kensington Gardens
Brighton
East Sussex BN1 4AL

Ms Sophie Gudgeon 029 2031 2400
Owner/Buyer
Pussy Galore
18 High Street Arcade
Cardiff CF10 1BB

Ms Amanda Cook 01932 866636
Owner/Buyer
Questa
49 High Street
Cobham
Surrey, UK KT11 3DP

Mr Jonathan Wells 01932 866636
Owner/Buyer
Questa
49 High Street
Cobham
Surrey, UK KT11 3DP

\

Judy/Dillon Ross 0207 385 7342
Owner/Buyer
Questionaire
141 Greyhound Road
London, UK W6 8NJ

Ms Rachel Tolhurst 01440 892 617
Buyer/Owner
Rachel Tolhurst
2 Ely Court, Royal Victoria Place
Tunbridge Wells
Kent TN1 2SP
E-mail: Rachel@tolhurst.co.uk

Ms Rebecca Junger 01491 413 737
Buyer
Rebecca
The Old Armistace
33 Hart Street Henley - on - Thames
Oxfordshire, UK RG9 2AR

Ms Belinda Robbins 01530 412020
Owner/Buyer
Rebellion
53 Market Street
Ashby De La Zouch
UK LE65 1AG

Mr Ben Driver +0 (778) 111-7726
Owner/Buyer
Red Ape
16 Le Pollet
St Peter Port
Guernsey CHANNEL ISLANDS

E-mail : redapeclothing@googlemail.com
www. redapeclothing.com

Ms Lesley Wickings 01534 617386
Owner/Buyer
Renaissance
26 Halkett Street
St Helier
Jersey JE2 4WJ

Ms Beverley Gough 01628 527176
Owner/Buyer
Repertoire
5-7 Gregories Road
Beaconsfield
Buckinghamshire HP9 1HG

Ms Lucy Shepherd 01202 540440
Buyer
Richmond Classics
UNIT 5 Branksome Business Park
Bourne Valley Road, Poole
Dorset BH12 1DW

Mr Dominic Riley 01482 868903
Owner/Buyer
11 Northbar Within
 Humberside
HU17 8AP

Ms Danielle Barker 00612 9332 2124
Administration assistant 00612 9332 1950
Robby Ingham Stores
424- 428 Oxford Street
Paddington
NSW 2021, Australia
E-mail: danielle@robbyingham.com.au

Ms Marlene Mangioni 00 612 9332 2124
Womenswear Buyer 00 612 9332 1950
Robby Ingham Stores
424 - 428 Oxford Street
Paddington
NSW 2021, Australia
E-mail : marlene@robbyingham>com.au

Ms Roberta Williamson 01202 470 346
Buyer
Roberta
1 Church Street
Christchurch
Dorset BH23 1BW

Ms Katie . 003 (531) 670-4007
Manager/Buyer
Rococo
1 The Westbury Shopping Mall
Harry Street
Dublin 2, Ireland

Ms Maria Dahlback 01534 733658
Buyer
Roulette Woman
15 Beresford Street
St Helier
Jersey JE2 4WY

Ms Clair Rous
Owner/Buyer
Rous Iland members boutique +0 (845) 003-8945
45 Clarges Street
Mayfair
London W1J 7EP
E-mail: Kara@rousiland.com

Ms Roz Clarke 01753 858517
Owner/ Buyer
Roz Clarke
19 St Leonards Road
Windsor
Berks SL4 3BP

Sarah Spice
Owner/buyer 01328 738638
Ruby and Tallullah
Church House
Overy Road, Burnham Market
Norfolk PE31 8HH

Ms Rosemarie Caplin 01619 808504
Ladies Buyer
Sacs
5 High Bank, De La Hayes
Hale
Cheshire WA15 8DZ

Ms Sally Parsons 0207 471 4848
Owner/Buyer
Sally Parsons
610 Fulham Road
London, UK SW6 5RP

Ms Keiko Kim-Hindley 0207 278 4497
Owner/Buyer
Saloon
23 Arlington Way
London EC1

Mrs Maureen Norris 01482 341 082
Buyer
Samanthas Boutique
56 Chanterlands Avenue
East Yorkshire HU5 3TT

Clodaugh Shorten 00353 21 427 8080
Owner/Buyer
Samui
17 Drawbridge Street
Cork, Ireland
E-mail:clodaughatsamui@eircom.net

Mr Adam Jagger 01904 611001
Womenswear Buyer
Sarah Coggles
91 - 93 Low Petergate
York, UK YO1 7HY

Mrs Megan Scotney 0116 2559261
Owner/ Buyer
Scotney For Women
128 - 132 London Road
Leicester
Leicestershire, UK LE2 1EB

Mr Douglas Mcwhannell 0041 0 43 3119853
Owner/Buyer
Scottish Clan House
Segantinistrasse 49
Zurich, Switzerland CH-8049

Ms Rosie Adams 01437 769 206
Buyer
Seasons
Williamson House
Swan Square, Haverfordwest,
Pembrookshire SA61 2HD

Ms Tina Patel 0207 226 7076
Buyer
Sefton, 271 Upper Street
Islington
London N1 2UQ
E-mail Address: t.patel@seftonuk.com

Sefton 0207 226 9822
271 Upper Street
Islington
London N1 2UQ

E-mail : t.patel@seftonuk.com

Ms Debbie Bardell
Lingerie Buyer
Selfridges
400 Oxford Street
London W1A 1AB

Ms Anita Barr
Buying Director of Womenswear
Selfridges
400 Oxford Street
London W1A 1AB

Ms Christine Benson
Beauty Buyer 0800 123400
Selfridges
400 Oxford Street
London W1A 1AB
E-mail :Christine.Benson@selfridges.co.uk

Ms Perushka De-Zoysa 0800 123400
Buying Manager ladies Contemporary, Spirit, Casuals
Selfridges
Ladies Contemporary, Spirit, Casuals
400 Oxford Street
London W1A 1AB
E-mail : Perushka.DeZoysa@selfridges.co.uk

Ms Rachel Duffy c0800 123400
Buyer - Accessories
Selfridges
400 Oxford Street
London W1A 1AB
E-mail : rachel.duffy@selfridges.co.uk

Mr Sam El-Kabbany
Buying Assistant, Ladies designerwear 0800 123400
Selfridges
400 Oxford Street
London W1A 1AB

Ms Laura Larbalestier
Buying Manager - Designerwear 0800 123400
Selfridges
Designerwear
400 Oxford Street
London W1A 1AB

Mr Sebastian Manes
Director of Accessories 0800 123400
Selfridges
400 Oxford Street
London W1A 1AB
E-mail : sebastian.manes@selfridges.co.uk

Ms Rebecca Osei - Baidoo
Buying assistant ladies designerwear
Selfridges
Designerwear & Millinery
400 Oxford Street
London W1A 1AB

Ms Jill Robertson
Buying assistant ladies designerwear
Selfridges
400 Oxford Street
London W1A 1AB

Mrs Jayne Turnbull 01737 779 121
Owner/Buyer
Seventeen 71 Company
4 Oliver Place
Hawick
Scottish Borders TD9 9BG

Ms Caroline Fairnie 0208 767 1961
Owner/Buyer
Siena
18 Bellevue Road
London, UK SW17 7EG

Ms Belinda Sly 01780 482 870
Owner/Buyer
Sly
10 St Mary's Hill
Stamford
Lincolnshire PE9 2DP
E-mail:belinda.sly@btopenworld.com

Ms Moira Thompson 0141 357 2334
Owner/Buyer
Solo
181 Hyndland Road
Glasgow G12 9HT

Ms Lynne Gardner 01225 464 997
Owner/ Buyer
Square Designer Womenswear
5/6 Shires Yard
Bath
Avon BA1 1BZ
E-mail :squarebath@aol.com

Mrs Beverley Vanger 0207 586 8658
Womenswear Buyer
Square One
43 St Johns Wood High Street
London NW8 7NJ

Ms Debbie Buckley 01446 773776
Owner/Buyer
Square spots
70a Eastgate
Cowbridge
South Glamorgan, UK

Ms Julia Stevens 01590 689 800
Buyer
Stanwells
13 High Street
Lymington
Hampshire, UK SO41 9AA

Ms Hannah Jennings 01803 835 079
Owner/Buyer
Starburst Boutique
15a Foss Street
Dartmouth
Devon TQ6 9DR
E-mail : info@starburstboutique.com
www.starburstboutique.com

Ms Brix- Smith Start 0207 739 3636
Owner/Buyer
Start
59 Rivington Street
London, UK EC2A 3QQ

Ms Vera Elsom 01243 784 486
Buyer
Stephen Lawrence
1 St Martins Street
Chichester
West Sussex PO19 1NP

Ms Lauren .01727 845856
Ladieswear Buyer
Storage
25 George Street
St Albans
UK AL3 4ES

E-mail : lauren@storageclothing.co.uk

Mrs Irene Willis 01727 831 154
Owner/ Buyer
Strides
6 George Street
St Albans
Herts, UK AL3 4ER

Ms Alison Gupy 01935 817 555
Buyer
Studio 4
4 Cheapside
Sherborne
Dorset DT9 3PX

Ms Marselle Savage 0207 449 0616
Buyer
Studio 8 The Origin
83 Regents Park Road
London NW1 8UY

Mrs Jane/ David Bear
Owner/ Buyers 0208 567 1385
Stuff
7 The Green
High Street Ealing
London W5 5DA

Ms Louise Aiken 0207 229 5434
Buyer
Sub Couture
204 Kensington Park Road
London, UK W11 1NR

Mrs Jan Shutt 01706 215 495
Owner/ Buyer
Sunday Best
56b Bank Street
Rawtenstall, Rossendale
Lancashire, UK BB4 8DY

Ms Jackie Patterson 01224 624 950
Partner/Buyer
Swanky Modes
49 Rose Street
Aberdeen AB10 1UB

Ms Wendy Goody 01580 714310
Owner/Buyer
Swans
1 Imber Court
Cranbrook
Kent, UK TN17 3DF

Ms Jules Winstanley 0208 977 8492
Buyer
TCS
28 High Street
Teddington
Middlesex, UK TW11 8EW

Kirsty 01604 259889
Womens Buyer
Thackerays
251 - 255 Wellingborough Road
Northampton
NN1 4EN

Ms Carol Wasson 01920 465565
Buyer
The Closet
94 High Street
Ware
Herts SG12 9AP

Ms Cheryl Cohen 01625 530 998
Owner/ Buyer
The Clothes Shop
8 Gravel Lane
Wilmslow
Cheshire, UK SK9 6LA

Mr Andrew Ibi 0208 968 9095
Owner/Buyer
The Convenience Store
1a Hazelwood Tower
Golborne Gardens
London W10 5DT

Ms Sam Robinson 0207 727 6760
Buyer
The Cross
141 Portland Road
London, UK W11 4LR
E-mail : julie@thecrossshop.com

Ms Siobha Canegie 00 353 1 6795718
Buyer
The Design Centre
Top Floor
Powerscourt Townhouse Centre
59 South William Street
Dublin 2, Ireland

Ms Deryane Tadd 01727 853 577
Owner Buyer
The Dressing Room
6-8 High Street
St Albans
Herts AL3 4EL

Ms Chris Roberts 020 8761 3457
Manageress
The Dulwich Trader
9 - 11 Croxted Road
London SE21 8SZ

Mrs Julie Marks 01483 455 202
Owner/ Buyer
The Foundation
210 High Street
Guildford
Surrey, UK GU1 3JB

Ms Amanda Priest 01724 270214
Owner/ Buyer
The Gallery
97 Mary Street
Scunthorpe, UK DN15 6LB

Ms Helen Gregory - Osbourne
Owner/ Buyer
The Glasshouse
66 Peascod Street
Windsor
Berks SL4 1DE

Ms Wendy Suffield 01258 452880
Owner/Buyer
The Hambledon Gallery
40 - 44 Salisbury Street
Blandford
Dorset, UK DT11 7PR

Ms Dinah Hughes 01642 790 816
Ladieswear Buyer
The House
69 High Street
Yarm, UK TS15 9BH

Ms Gillian Bisset 01608 650242
Owner/ Buyer
The Linen Press
Hope House
Moreton In Marsh
Gloucs, UK GL56 OLH

The Shop At Bluebird 0208 351 3873
350 Kings Road
Chelsea
London SW3 5UU

Ms Lucy Benzecry 0207 243 6912
Owner/Buyer
The West Village
35 Kensington Park Road
London, UK W11 2EU

Manami Sloley 0207 823 7310
Buyer
Tokio
197 Westbourne Grove
London, UK W11

Mrs Anya/ Gunva Heaseman 01444 482337
Owner/ Buyers
Tollhouse
56 High Street
Lindfield
West Sussex RH16 2HL

Mr David Fairthorne 01242 257 325
Buyer
Trapeze
Unit 3
50 Regent Street, Cheltenham
Glouc GL50 1HA

Ms Kathryn Pick 01642 249989
Buyer
Triads Women
182 Linthorpe Road
Middlesborough TS1 3RF

Ms Laura Starbuck
Buyer 01273 673755
Tribeca
21 Bond Street
Brighton
East Sussex BN1 1RD

Ms Lesley Tarson 0207 730 6515
Buyer
Trilogy
33 Duke of York Square
London SW3 4LY
E-mail : jameslesley@mac.com

Ms Nell Graham 0131 557 4045
Owner/ Buyer
Troon
1 York Place
Edinburgh
Midlothian EH1 3EB

Ms Joan Taylor 0115 9470 189
Owner/ Buyer
Tutu
1 The exchange Arcade
Nottingham
UK NG1 2DD

Ms Muriel Scotchmere 01896 822 122
Owner/Buyer
Twelve Of Melrose
12 High Street
Melrose
Roxburghshire, TD6 9PA, Scotland
E-mail : muriel@twelveofmelrose.com

Ms Vicky Eggleston 0191 384 8500
Buyer
Van Mildert Women
19 - 21 Elvet Bridge
Durham DH1 3WA

Ms Vania Jesmond 01792 461 165
Owner/ Buyer
Vania Jesmond
89 Brynymor Road
Swansea
West Glamorgan, UK SA1 4JE

Ms Renate Beaumont 01865 552155
Owner/ Buyer
Vanilla
13 South Parade
Summertown
Oxford, UK OX2 7JN

Ms Debra Helliwell 01282 699797
Owner/Buyer
Velvet
5 King Edward Terrace
Gisburn Road, Barrowford
Lancashire BB9 8NJ

Ms Debra Helliwell 07974 926577
Owner/Buyer
Velvet of Lytham
5a Clifton Street
Lytham St Annes
Lancashire FY8 7EP

Ms Shirley Milne 01224 644 558
Owner/Buyer
Verdict
13 Thistle Street
Aberdeen AB10 1XZ

Ms Vicky Egglestone 01642 803302
Owner/Buyer
View Womenswear
71a High Street
Yarm
Cleveland, UK TS15 9BG

Mrs Serena Hunter 01420 82225
Owner/Buyer
Vintage Violet
51 High Street
Hampshire GU34 1AW

Mrs Caroline Slinder 0207 586 8600
Buyer
Viva
72 St Johns Wood High Street
London NW8 7SH

Ms Vivian Aygun 01534 870511
Womenswear Buyer
Voisins
King Street
St Helier
Jersey, UK

Ms Suzie Faux 0207 494 1131
Owner/Buyer
Wardrobe
42 Conduit Street
London W1S 2HY

Mr Ian Waud 01635 528 000
Buyer/Owner
Waud Ladieswear
59 Northbrook Street
Newbury
Berkshire RG14 1AN

Ms Sally White 01834 860 664
Buyer
White
3 High Street
Narbeth
Dyfed SA67 7AR

Ms Ann Wiberg 0208 987 9715
Owner/Buyer
Wild- Swans
14 Devonshire Road
London W4 2HD
E-mail :info@wild-swans.com

Mrs Sue Jackson 01392 490031
Owner/ Buyer
Willys
24 Gandy Street
Exeter
Devon, UK EX4 3LF

Mr Samir Ceric
0207 229 5698
Owner/Buyer
Wolf & Badger
46 Ledbury Road
Nottinghill
London W11 2AB
E-mail : info@wolfandbadger.com
www.wolfandbadger.com

Ms Zoe Knight 0207 229 5698
Owner/designer/Buyer
Wolf & Badger
46 Ledbury Road
Nottinghill
 London W11 2AB
E-mail :info@wolfandbadger.com
www.wolfandbadger.com

Mr David Keveren 029 2023 2171
Buyer
Woodies Emporium
22-26 Morgan Arcade
Cardiff CS10 1AF

Mr Garry Johnson 01622 766 262
Buyer
Woods
77 Bank Street
Maidstone
Kent ME14 1SJ

Ms Jemima Johnson 01258 488 766
Owner/Buyer
Wren
17 Salisbury Street
Blandford Forum
Dorset DT11 7AU

Ms Sunna Yates 0207 229 5884
Owner/Buyer
Yates Buchanan
33 Pembridge Road
NottingHill
London W11 3HG
E-mail :info@yatesbuchanan.com

Ms Dorothy Thomas 01335 342095
Owner/ Buyer
Young Ideas
5 St John Street
Ashbourne
Derbyshire, UK DE6 1DP
E-mail :style@young-ideas.demon.co.uk

Lindsey Halligan 01245 356 358
Buyer
Zagger Woman
14-26 Baddow Road
Chelmsford
Essex, UK CM2 ODG

Ms Michelle Johnson 01279 422 802
Buyer
Zee & Co
221 - 223 High Street
Loughton
Essex, UK IG10 1BB

Menswear Directory

Mr Martin Schneider
Accent
11 - 20 Queens Arcade
Briggate
Leeds LS1 6LF
0113 234 6767
Web site: www.accentclothing.com

Mr Bashir Mohammed
Owner/Buyer
American Pie
15 The Broadway
Ealing
London W5 2NH
0208 567 2203

Ms Sue Tahran
Oner/Buyer
American Retro
35 Old Compton Street
Soho
London W1D 5JX
0207 734 6885
Web site: www.americanretrolondon.com

Mr Tim Guy
Owner/Buyer
Andrew Gardner
2-4 Tanyard
Tring Road, Wendover
Buckinghamshire HP22 6ND
0129 662 5488

Mr Andrew Watson
Owner/Buyer
Andrew Watson Menswear
11 Upper Queen Street
Belfast
Northern Ireland BT1 2NE
02890 243412
E-mail Address:info@andrewwatsonfashion.com
Website:www.andrewwatsonfashion.com

Mr Andrew & Duncan Mckenzie
Owner/Buyers
Aphrodite 1994
8 Vine Place
Sunderland SR1 3NE
0191 567 5898
E-mail Address:enquiries@aphrodite1994.co.uk
Websitewww.aphrodite1994.com

Mr Adam Clarke
Owner/Buyer
ARC
42 Blandford Street
Sunderland SR1 3JH
0191 5674305
E-mail Address:info@arcjeans.co.uk
Website:www.arcmenswear.com

Mr Lawrence Taylor
Owner/Buyer
Aristocrat
The Chantry
2-4 Hadlam Road, Bishops Stortford
Hertfordshire CM23 2QR
01279 652019

Mr Luke Dennison
Owner/Buyer
Ashes Menswear Ltd
86 Old Christchurch Road
Bournemouth
Dorset BH1 1LR
01202 554809
E-mail Address   info@ashesmenswear.co.uk
Web site   www.ashesmenswear.co.uk

Mr Mel Pilkington
Owner Buyer
Aspecto Clothing Co Ltd
2nd Floor Sevendale House
7 Dale Street
Manchester M1 1JB
0161 747 2318
E-mail Address   buyonline@aspecto.co.uk
Web site   www.aspecto.co.uk

Mr Richard McLaughlin
Owner/Buyer
Attic
The Academy Centre
Belmont Street
Aberdeen AB10 1LB
01224 644000
Web site   www.atticclothing.com

Mr John White
Owner/Buyer
Badger Clothing
25-26 Bond Street
Brighton
East Sussex BN1 1RD
01273 722 245
Web site   www.badgerclothing.co.uk

Mr Dan Palmer
Mens Assistant Buyer
Bank
Hollinsbrook Way,
Pilsworth, Bury
Lancashire BL9 8RR
0161 767 7157

Mr Wayne Selt
Owner/Buyer
Baron Jon
Unit 5 Woodside Industrial Estate
Works Road, Letchworth
Hertfordshire SG6 1LA
0845 034 4788
E-mail Address   enquiries@baronjon.com
Web site   www.baronjon.com

Mr Marc Granditer
Managing Director
Base Retail Ltd
Unit 2 Woodford Trading Estate
 Southend Road, Woodford Green
Essex IG8 8HF
0208 551 4455
Web site   www.basefashion.co.uk

The Menswear Buyer
Bellusci
52 Bank Street
Rawtenstall
BB4 8DY
01706 222752
E-mail Address   info@bellusci.co.uk

Mr Rupert Adams
Owner/Buyer
Benets
3 Market Place
Southwell
Notts NG25 OHE
01636 813894
E-mail Address   info@benets.co.uk
Web site   www.benets.co.uk

Ms Jane McCoy
Owner/Buyer
Bibi & Mac
56 Fore Street
Salcombe
Devon TQ8 8ET
01548 843595

Black's
1 Pepper Street
Newcastle -under-Lyme
ST5 1PR
01782 616150

Ms Joan Kershaw
Owner/Buyer
Blueberries
101 Topping Street
Blackpool
Lancashire FY1 3AA
01253 622358
E-mail Address   info@blueberries-online.com
Web site   www.blueberries-online.com

Mr Lee Warraner
The Menswear Buyer
Bolo
18 Saville Street
Hull
North Humberside HU1 3EF
01482 586620
Web site   www.bolo.co.uk

Mr Kelvin Gill
Owner/Buyer
Brother 2 Brother
The Harlequin
Town Centre
Watford WD17 2TA
01923 211882

Ms Caroline Burstein
Creative Director
Browns
23-27 South Molton Streer
London W1K 5RD
0207 514 0000
Web site   www.brownsfashion.com

Mr Anthony O'Hagan
Buyer
Camp Hobson
7-11 Northbrook Street
Newbury
Berkshire RG14 1DN
01635 523523
E-mail Address   mail@camphobson.co.uk
Web site   www.camphobson.co.uk

Mr David Godfrey
Owner/Buyer
Chameleon Menswear
Unit 31
West Orchards
Coventry CV1 1QT
0246 550000
E-mail Address info@chameleonmenswear.co.uk

Mr Darren Conway
Buying Director
Choice Ltd
PO Box 2892
Romford RM7 1LR
0845 271 9905

Mr Ghulam Mustafa
The Menswear Buyer
Circle
34-40 Westgate
Huddersfield HD1 1NX
0148 4435271

Mr John Brown
Owner/Buyer
Cody Menswear
111- 113 Fore Street
Exeter
Devon EX4 3JF
01392 213880
Web site	www.codymenswear.com

Mr Frank de-Jesus
Menswear Buyer
Collections Group
1 Bath Street
St Helier
Jersey JE2 4ST
01534 519111
E-mail Address	frank@collectionsgroup.com
Web site	www.collectionsgroup.com

Ms Clare Adkins
Buyer/Owner
Collen & Clare
25 Market Place
Southwold
Suffolk IP18 6ED
01502 724823

Ms Vanessa Collen
Buyer
Collen & Clare
25 Market Place
Southwold,
Suffolk IP18 6ED
01502 724 823
Web site	www.collenand clare.com

Mr John Cook
The Menswear Buyer
Colonel Mustard
23 Penn Street
Cabot Circus
Bristol BS1 3AU
0117 927 6060
E-mail Address info@colonelmustardfashion.co.uk
Web site www.colonelmustardfashion.co.uk

Mr Mark Higgs
Owner/Buyer
Common
161 Wellingborough Road
Northampton
NN1 4DX

Mr Kevin Lonie
Owner/Buyer
Concept Clothing
The Academy Shopping Centre
Belmont Street
Aberdeen AB10 1LB
01224 635268
E-mail Address   esales@conceptclothing.co.uk
Web site   www.conceptclothing.co.uk

Ms Emily Dyson
Owner/Buyer
Couverture and the Garbstore
188 Kensington Park Road
Portobello
London W11 2ES
0207 229 2178
E-mail Address info@couvertureandthegarbstore.com
Web site www.couvertureandthegarbstore.com

Mr Daniel Jenkins
Owner/Buyer
Daniel Jenkins
94 Monnow Street
Monmouth NP25 3EQ

E-mail Address   daniel@danieljenkins.co.uk
Web site   www.danieljenkins.co.uk

Mr Matt Horstead
Owner/Buyer
Dartagnan Menswear
56a East Street
Chichester
West Sussex PO19 1JG
01243 539 491
E-mail Address   info@dartagnanmenswear.co.uk
Web site   www.dartagnanmenswear.co.uk

Mr David Corry
Owner/Buyer
Davicore Clothing Ltd
The Old Bank
16 High Street
Doncaster DN1 1EX
01302 344105
E-mail Address   sales@davicoreclothing.com
Web site   www.davicoreclothing.com

Mr James Venning
Buyer
Debenhams PLC
1 Welbeck Street
London W1G 0AA
0207 408 3544

Ms Lyn Knights
Owner/Buyer
Denny Of Southwold
11 Market Place
Southwold
Suffolk   IP18 6EA
01502 722372
E-mail Address   info@dennyofsouthwold.co.uk
Web site   www.dennyofsouthwold.co.uk

The Menswear Buyer
Designerwear Online Ltd
Clifton House
Clifton Road
Blackpool   FY4 4QA
0844 3356744
E-mail Address   info@designerwear.co.uk
Web site   www.designerwear.co.uk

Mr Gerald Bailey
Owner/Buyer
Diffusion
68 Victoria Street
Wolverhampton   WV1 3NX
01902 716 762
Web site   www.diffusiononline.co.uk

Mr Mark Howard
Owner/Buyer
Disorder Ltd
Unit 1 Imperial House
14 Needless Alley
Birmingham   B2 5AE
0121 643 21 31
E-mail Address   enquiries@disorder-uk.com
Web site   www.disorder-uk.co

Alex .
Buyer
Diverse Womenswear & Menswear
294 Upper Street
Islington
London N1 2TU
0207 3598877
E-mail Address   alex@diverseclothing.com
Web site   www.diverseclothing.com

The Menswear Buyer
Dome Clothing
16 Nevill Street
Southport
Merseyside PR9 OBX
0 (170) 454-8099
E-mail Address domeclothingsales@hotmail.com
Web site   www.domeclothing.co.uk

Mr Rei Kawakubo
Owner/Buyer
Dover Street Market
17 - 18 Dover Street
Mayfair
London W1S 4LT
0207 518 0680
E-mail Address   info@doverstreetmarket.com
Web site   www.doverstreetmarket.com

Mr Llyas Patel
Buyer/Owner
Duffer Menswear
9 Fishergate
Preston
Lancashire PR1 2EJ
01772 254811
E-mail Address info@duffermenswearonline.co.uk
Web site   www.duffermenswear.co.uk

The Menswear Buyer
Elements
12 Lower Goat Lane
Norwich
NR2 1EL
01603 618 661
E-mail Address   info@elementsclothing.co.uk
Web site   www.elementsclothing.co.uk

Mr Neil Symington
Owner/Buyer
Eleven- Men and Women
56 John Street
Sunderland SR1 1QH
0191 564 1155
Web site   www.eleven-shop.co.uk

Mr John Parker
Owner/Buyer
End Clothing
4-6 High Bridge
Newcastle Upon Tyne NE1 1EN
0191 261 9327
E-mail Address   info@endclothing.co.uk
Web site   www.endclothing.co.uk

Mr John Parker
Owner/Buyer
End Clothing
4-6 High Bridge
Newcastle Upon Tyne NE1 1EN
0191 261 9327
E-mail Address	info@endclothing.co.uk
Web site	www.endclothing.co.uk

Mr P. Khatkar
Buyer/Owner
Escape Menswear
14-16 Spring Street
Portsmouth PO1 4AA
023 9275 5107

Mr Andrew Maloney
Owner/Buyer
Eton Clothing Ltd
65-67 Division Street
Sheffield S1 4GE
0114 2724487
E-mail Address	shop@eton-clothing.co.uk
Web site	www.eton-clothing.co.uk

Mr Darren Comerford
Owner/Buyer
Fallen Hero
8 Cole Street
Scunthorpe
Lincolnshire DN15 6QZ
01724 855688
Web site	www.fallenhero.co.uk

Mr Blair Finlay
Owner/Buyer
Finlay Grant
14 High Street
Melrose
Scotland TD6 9PA
01896 822042
Web site   www.finlaygrant.com

Mr Tim Bower
Menswear Buyer
Flannels Group Ltd
Unit 6 Waterside
Wharfside Commerce Park, Trafford Park
Manchester M17 1WD
0161 931 2593
E-mail Address   info@flannelsfashion.com

Mr Tim Lancaster
Senior Buyer
Flannels Group Ltd
Unit 6 Waterside
Wharfside Commerce Park, Trafford Park
Manchester M17 1WD
0161 931 2593

Mr Peter Sadler
Owner/Buyer
Fluke
1.25-1.26 Street Nicholas Centre
Sutton
Surrey SM1 1AW
0208 661 9358

Mr Malcolm Bird
Owner/Buyer
Frank Bird
26/30 The Arcade
Barnsley
South Yorkshire S70 2QN
01226 203891
E-mail Address   barnsley@frankbird.com
Web site   www.frankbird.com

Ms Joe Lowcock
Owner/Buyer
Fusion
81 Friargate Walk
The Mall St George Shopping Centre,
Preston PR1 2NQ
01772 887900
E-mail Address   info@fusionfashion.co.uk
Web site   www.fusionfashion.co.uk

Mr Andy Rourke
Owner/Buyer
G2 Lifestyle
Unit 2 Scotshaw Industrial Estate
Branch Road, Lower Darwen
Lancs BB3 0PR
01254 582944
E-mail Address   info@g2lifestyle.com
Web site   www.g2lifestyle.com

Mr Peter Lake
Owner/Buyer
Garment Quarter
25 Penn Street
Bristol BS1 3AU
+0 (117) 329-4405
E-mail Address   info@garmentquarter.com
Web site   www.garmentquarter.com

Mr Giancarlo Ricci
Owner/Buyer
Giancarlo Ricci
40 Bold Street
Liverpool L1 4DS

Web site   www.giancarloricci.co.uk

Mr Giulio Cinque
Owner/Buyer
Giulio
24-32 King Street
Cambridge CB1 1LN
01223 316100

Mr Ian Craigie
Owner/Buyer
Goodstead Ltd
76 Rose Street
Edinburgh EH2 2NN
0131 228 2846

Mr Nathan Good
Owner/Buyer
Gravity Menswear
Moseley's Yard, Shropshire Street
Audlem
Cheshire CW3 0AL
01270 811611
E-mail Address   info@gravity-menswear.co.uk
Web site   www.gravity-menswear.co.uk

The Menswear Buyer
Grewaiz Partners International
35-37 Uxbridge Road
Shepherds Bush
London W12 8LH
0208 735 1801

The Menswear Buyer
Hatters
11-13 White Lion Street
Norfolk
Norwich NR2 1QA
01603 626469

Mr Russell Scott-Lawson
Owner/Buyer
Hawkes Essentials
35-39 Morgan Arcade
Cardiff CF10 1AF
029 2037 3780
E-mail Address enquiries@hawkesessentials.com
Web site   www.hawkesessentials.com

Mr Oscar Pinto-Hervia
Hervia Bazaar
40 Spring Gardens
Manchester M2 1EN
0161 835 2777
E-mail Address   mstore@herviabazaar.com
Web site   www.herviabazaar.com

Mr Everton Campbell
Owner/Buyer
Hip
9 & 14 Thorntons Arcade
Leeds
West Yorkshire LS1 6LQ
0113 242 4617
E-mail Address   info@hipleeds.com

Mr James Brown
Owner/Buyer
HOSTEM
41-43 Redchurch Street
London E2 7DJ
0207 739 9733
E-mail Address   info@hostem.co.uk
Web site   www.hostem.co.uk

Mr Kevin Rogers
Branded Menswear Buyer
House of Fraser
27 Baker Street
London W1U 8AH
0207 828 1000
E-mail Address   krogers@hof.co.uk

Mr Lee Simpson
Buying Director
Hugh Harris
13 High Street
Woking
Surrey GU21 6BL
01483 888855
E-mail Address customerservices@hughharris.co.uk
Web site   www.hughharrisshop.co.uk

Mr Mark Hurley
Owner/Buyer
Hurley
10 South Street
The Rock
Bury BL9 ONN

Mr Mark Hurley
Owner/Buyer
Hurley Menswear
83 Piccadilly
Manchester
Lancashire M1 2BZ
0161 2281490

The Menswear Buyer
Ideology Menswear
Unit 11 The Forum
127-129 Devonshire Street
Sheffield S3 7SB
0114 2723482
Web site   www.ideologyboutique.co.uk

The Menswear Buyer
IKON
13 Tunsgate Square
Guildford
Surrey GU1 3QZ
01483 531263

Mr Martyn Sole
Buyer
Infinities
86 George Street
Altringham
Cheshire WA14 1RF
0161 929 6074

Mr Jeremy Clayton
Owner/Buyer
Javelin
37 Abbeygate Street
Bury St Edmunds
Suffolk IP33 1LW
01284 754559
Web site	www.javelinonline.co.uk

Mr Andrew Hobbs
Owner/Buyer
Jeremy Hobbs Fine Menswear
1 Holly Parade
High Street Cobham
Surrey KT11 3EE
01932 865700
Web site	www.jeremyhobbs.co.uk

Mr John Nooney
Buyer/Owner
John Anthony
Unit 4 The Onega Centre
Upper Bristol Road
Bath BA1 3AG
01225 442856

Mr John Nooney
Owner/Buyer
John Anthony
Head Office
Unit 4 The Onega Centre
Upper Bristol Road
Bath BA1 3AG
01225 442856
E-mail Address   customerservice@john-anthony.com
Web site   www.john-anthony.com

Mr John Goodwin
Owner/Buyer
John Goodwin
95 Peascod Street
Windsor
Berkshire SL4 1DH
01753 866116
E-mail Address enquiries@johngoodwin-online.com
Web site   www.johngoodwin-online.com

Mr Carsten Skovgaard
Branded Menswear Buyer
John Lewis
E-mail Address: carsten_skovgaard@johnlewis.co.uk

Mr Roger Kingsley
Owner/Buyer
Jonathan Trumbull
5 St Stephen's Street
Norwich
Norfolk NR1 3QL
01603 629876

Mr Craig Oliver
Menswear Buyer
Jules B
46 Acorn Road
Jesmond
Newcastle Upon Tyne NE2 2DJ
0191 281 7855

The Menswear Buyer
Keith James Menswear
124-128 Town Street
Horsforth
Leeds LS18 4AQ
0113 2582605
E-mail Address   keithjames1@live.co.uk

Mr Dave Doneky
Owner/Buyer
Kingsley Clothing
38 Holmeside
Sunderland
0191 567 7377
E-mail Address   kingsley@kingsley1.com
Web site   www.kingsleyclothing.com

Mr Gavin Colwill
Owner/Buyer
Kiosk 78
B8-The Balcony
Corn Exchange
Call Lane
Leeds LS1 7BR
0113 2443934
E-mail Address   info@kiosk78.co.uk
Web site   www.kiosk78.co.uk

Mr Tony Young
Manager
Le monde menswear
56 Victoria Street
Wolverhampton
West Midlands WV1 3NX
01902 714448
E-mail Address   info@lemondemenswear.co.uk

The Menswear Buyer
Leonard Silver
51 Savile Street
Hull HU1 3EA
01482 223025
Web site   www.leonardsilver.com

The Menswear Buyer
Life Clothing Limited
Town Street
Horsforth
Leeds LS18 4AQ
01132 582605
E-mail Address   admin@lifeclothing.co.uk
Web site   www.lifeclothing.co.uk

Mr Aziz Abidat
Owner/Buyer
Made Man
46 Salusbury Road
Queens Park
London NW6 6NN
0207 625 9366
E-mail Address   info@mademanclothing.com

Ms Angela Earnshaw
Buyer
Mainline Menswear
Bakers court
Hopper Hill Road,
Scarborough YO11 3YS
01723 379900

Ms Angela Earnshaw
Menswear Buyer
Mainline Menswear
10a Huntriss Row
Scarborough
North Yorkshire YO11 2ED
01723 379900

The Menswear Buyer
Manhattan
1 Bridge Street
Hemel Hampstead
Hertfordshire HP1 1EG
01442 250 649
E-mail Address   hemel@manhattan-menswear.co.uk
Web site   www.manhattan-menswear.co.uk

The menswear Buyer
Manhattan Menswear
242 High Street
Slough
Berkshire SL1 1JU
01753 537820
E-mail Address   slough@manhattan-menswear.co.uk
Web site www.manhattan- menswear.co.uk

Mr Forrest Rosscraig
Owner/Buyer
Manifesto
78 Commercial Street
Dundee
Angus DD1 2AP
01382 201 527

Ms Frances Card
Commercial Director
Matches Head Office
15a Welmar Mews
154 Clapham Park Road
London SW4 7DD

Mr Glenn Baughan
The Menswear Buyer
Maze Clothing Ltd
7a Riverside Place
St James Street, Taunton
Somerset TA1 1JH
0-1823 254704
Web site   www.mazeclothing.co.uk

Mr Michael Cleary
Owner/Buyer
Michael Barrie
20 Duke Street
Dublin 2
00353 671 5265

Mr Nigel Bird
Owner/Buyer
Michael Chell
188 High Street
Guildford
Surrey GU1 3HW
01483 457735

Mr Jay Linturn
Owner/Buyer
Michael Chell
6 - 14 St Leonards Road
Windsor
Berkshire SL4 3BW
01753 862589

Mr Richard Blackburn
Owner/Buyer
Michael Stewart
9-13 Brook Street
Selby
North Yorkshire YO8 4AL
01757 703139
E-mail Address   sales@michaelstewart.co.uk
Web site   www.michaelstewart.co.uk

Mr Paul Khatkar
Owner/Buyer
Mirage Menswear
111 Commercial Road
Portsmouth PO1 1BU
023 9286 1732

Mr Terry Betts
Senior Buyer
Mr Porter

Mr Reece Crisp
Assistant Buyer - Mens Contemporary
Mr Porter

Mr Sam Lobban
Contemporary Buyer
Mr Porter

Ms Ciara Flood
Assistant Buyer
Mr Porter.com

Mr Stephen Peters
Owner/Buyer
Neckline
164 Fortis Green Road
London N10 3DU
0208 442 0006
E-mail Address   infonecklineltd@aol.com

Mr Nigel Holmes
Owner/Buyer
Nigel Holmes
3 Park Street
Lytham
Lancashire FY8 5LU
01253 739 531
E-mail Address   info@nigel-holmes.co.uk
Web site   www.nigel-holmes.co.uk

Mr Phil Goodfellow
Owner/Buyer
 Northern Threads
14 Ocean Roads
South Shields
Tyne and Wear NE33 2HZ
0191 4547358
E-mail Address   info@northernthreads.co.uk
Web site   www.northernthreads.co.uk

Mr Steve Sanderson
Owner/Buyer
Oi Polloi
63 Thomas Street
Manchester M4 1LQ
0161 831 7870
E-mail Address   buying@oipolloi.com
Web site   www.oipolloi.com

Mr John Devaney
Owner/Buyer
Originals
109/111 Blackburn Road
Accrington
Lancashire BB5 1JJ
01254 388226
E-mail Address   info@originalsclothing.co.uk
Web site   www.originalsclothing.co.uk

The Menswear Buyer
Palmer Menswear
771 Fulham Road
Hammersmith & Fulham
London SW6 5HA
0207 384 2044
0207 371 8130

Mr Steve Slack
Owner/Buyer
Petrus Design
14 High Street
Saffron Walden
Essex CB10 1AY
01799 525313
Web site   www.petrusdesign.co.uk

Mr Philip Browne
Owner/Buyer
Philip Browne Menswear
1 Guildhall Hill
Norwich
NR2 1JH
01603 664886
E-mail Address info@philipbrownemenswear.co.uk
Web site www.philipbrownemenswear.co.uk

Mr Garth Coverdale
Director
Pilot
36 - 38 Silver Street
Leicester LE1 5ET
0116 262 8200
Web site   www.netclothing.net

Mr Paul Platt
Owner/Buyer
Pockets
Casual Shop
7a The square
Shrewsbury SY1 1LA
01743 353993
Web site   www.pockets.co.uk

Mrs Rita Britton
Owner
Pollyanna
14-16 Market Hill
Barnsley
South Yorkshire S70 2QE
01226 291 665
Web site   www.pollyanna.com

Mr Steve Davies
Owner/Buyer
Present
140 Shoreditch High Street
London E1 6JE
0207 033 0500
E-mail Address   info@present-london.com

Mr Edward Pritchard
Owner/Buyer
Pritchards
9 King Street
Hereford HR4 9BW
01432 272346
E-mail Address   web@pritchards.co.uk
Web site   www.pritchards.co.uk

Mr B. Ajoodanpour
Owner/Buyer
Profile
27 Dukes Lane
Brighton BN1 1BG
01273 733 086
E-mail Address profileonline@profilebrighton.co.uk
Web site   www.profilebrighton.co.uk

Mr Steve Cochrane
Buyer/Owner
Psyche
175-187 Linthorpe Road
Middlesborough
Cleveland TS1 4AG
01642 707286
E-mail Address   info@psyche.co.uk
Web site   www.psyche.co.uk

Mr Mark Hardeman
Owner/Buyer
Ragazzi
37 - 39 St Georges Crescent
Wrexham LL13 8DB
01978 264 460
E-mail Address   sales@ragazziclothing.co.uk
Web site   www.ragazziclothing.co.uk

Mr James Mathews
Owner/Buyer
Ran
7-8 St Annes's Arcade
St Anne's Square
Manchester M2 7HQ
0161 877 6342
E-mail Address   info@ranshop.co.uk
Web site   www.ranshop.co.uk

Mr Ben Driver
Owner/Buyer
Red Ape Clothing
16 The Pollet
St Peter Port
Guernsey GY1 1WH
01481 721847
E-mail Address   ben@redapeclothing.com
Web site   www.redapeclothing.com

The Menswear Buyer
Red Square
159 Linthorpe Road
Middlesbrough TS1 4AG
01642 254825
E-mail Address   info@redsquareclothing.co.uk
Web site   www.redsquareclothing.co.uk

Mrs Beverly Gough
Owner/Buyer
Repertoire
5-7 Gregories Road
Beaconsfield
Buckinghamshire HP9 1HG
01494 681 655
Web site   www.repertoirefashion.co.uk

Mr Mark Gough
Owner/Buyer
Repertoire
6 & 8 High Street
Marlow
Buckinghamshire SL7 1AW
01628 476996
Web site   www.repertoirefashion.co.uk

Mr Steven Grady
Menswear Buyer
Republic Retail - Head Office
2100 Century Way
Leeds
West Yorkshire LS15 8ZB
0113 390 0900

Mr Scott Macrae
Head of external brands
Republic Retail- Head Office
2100 Century Way
Leeds
West Yorkshire LS15 8ZB
0113 390 0900
E-mail Address   scott.macrae@republic.co.uk
Web site   www.republic.co.uk

Mr Nick Reaver
Owner/Buyer
Resonate
97a High Street
Haborne
Birmingham B17 9NR
01214 261300
E-mail Address   info@resonatemenswear.com
Web site   www.reasonatemenswear.com

Mr Rob Pritchard
Owner/Buyer
Resurrection
17-19 Bold Street
Liverpool L1 4DN
0151 709 2676
E-mail Address   info@resurrection-online.com
Web site   www.resurrection-online.com

Mr David Moss
Owner/Buyer
Richard Gelding
27 North Audley Street
Mayfair
London W1K 6WU
0207 629 0618
E-mail Address   info@geldingmenswear.co.uk
Web site   www.geldingmenswear.co.uk

Mr Keith McNicol
Owner/Buyer
Richmond Classics
7a -11 Richmond Hill
Bournemouth BH2 6HE
01202 290992
Web site   www.richmondclassics.com

Mr Raymond Riley
Owner/Buyer
Riley's
11 North Bar Within
Beverley
East Yorkshire HU17 8AP
01482 868903

Robert Fuller
12 & 14 High Street
Banstead
Surrey SM7 2LJ
01737 356789
Web site   www.robert-fuller.co.uk

Mr Russell Jones
Owner/Buyer
Robinsons
2 South Parade
Bawtry
Doncaster DN10 6JH
01302 711477
E-mail Address   info@robinsonsofbawtry.com
Web site   www.robinsonsofbawtry.com

Mr Rowan Hines
Owner/Buyer
Room 14 Menswear
14 George Street
Ashton - Under - Lyne
Lancashire OL6 6AQ
0161 330 5506
 E-mail Address   admin@room14menswear.co.uk
Web site   www.room14menswear.co.uk

Mr Dave Kerr
Owner/Buyer
Sa-Kis
Unit 11, 3rd Floor
4 Orchard Square
Sheffield S1 2FB
0114 3030135

Mr Shami Chadha
Owner/Buyer
Sage
41 Church Street
Enfield
Middlesaex EN2 6AJ
0208 366 9624

Mr Mike Simpkin
Owner/Buyer
Sakks Menswear
Shamrock Quay
William Street
Southampton S014 5QL
023 8063 7892
E-mail Address   sakksmenswear@btconnect.com
Web site   www.sakksmenswear.co.uk

Mr David Whitby
Owner/Buyer
Samuel Pepys
31 High Street
St Peter Port, Guernsey
Channel Islands GY1 2JX
01481 727616
E-mail Address   info@samuelpepys.com
Web site   www.samuelpepys.com

Mr Mark Bage
Owner/Buyer
Sarah Coggles
91-93 Low Petergate
York YO1 7HY
01904 611001
E-mail Address   contact@coggles.com

Ms Katherine Taylor
Owner/Buyer
Scene
79 Main Street
Dickens Heath, Solihull
West Midlands B90 1UB
0121 733 6005
E-mail Address   enquiries@scenemenswear.com
Web site   www.scenemenswear.com

Mr Jordan Rowlin
Owner/Buyer
Seasons Clothing
7-11 Cross Arcade
Victoria Quarter
Leeds LS1 6AZ
0113 234 5907
E-mail Address   info@seasonsclothing.co.uk

Mr Ben Elsdale
Owner/Buyer
Sefton
196 Upper Street
London N1 1RQ
0207 226 7076
Website: www.seftonfashion.com

Mr Nad Ahmed
Owner/Buyer
Serene Order
41 Drury Lane
Solihull
West Midlands B91 3BP
0121 711 6942
E-mail Address   info@sereneorder.com
Web site   www.sereneorder.com

Mr Michael Haworth
Buyer
Shop Direct Home Shopping Limited
Skyways House
Speke Road, Speke
Liverpool L70 1AB
0151 432 4085

Mr Patrick Ritchie
Owner/Buyer
Signature
349 Union Street
Aberdeen AB11 6BT
01224 210050
Web site   www.signature-menswear.com

Mr Giles Henderson
Owner/Buyer
Six Whiting Street
6 Whiting Street
Bury St Edmunds
IP33 1NX
01284 769886
E-mail Address   sales@sixwhitingstreet.co.uk
Web site   www.sixwhitingstreet.co.uk

Mr Darren Evans
Owner/Buyer
Smart Ass Menswear
27 High Street
Conwy
Conwy LL32 8DE
01492 585125
Web site   www.smartassmenswear.co.uk

The Menswear Buyer
Square 1
51a St John's Wood High Street
St John's Wood
London NW8 7NJ
0208 586 8658

Mr Philip Start
Owner/Buyer
Start
42-44 Rivington Street
London EC2A 3QP
0207 033 3951
E-mail Address   buying@start-london.com
Web site   www.start-london.com

Mr Alan Freeman
Owner/Buyer
Steem Menswear
140 High Street North
East Ham
 E6 2HT
0208 471 6235
E-mail Address   info@steemmenswear.co.uk
Web site   www.steammenswear.co.uk

Mr Jay Saklani
Owner/Buyer
Storage Menswear
Chapel Street
Luton
Bedfordshire LU1 5SA
01582 488086
Web site   www.storageclothing.co.uk

Mr Ravi Grewal
Owner/Buyer
Stuarts
35-37 Uvbridge Road
Shepherds Bush
London W12 8LH
0208 735 1801
Web site   www.stuartslondon.com

Mr Douglas Mckinna
Owner/Buyer
Swish
22 Victoria Street
Edinburgh EH1 2JW
0131 220 0615
E-mail Address   help@swishlife.co.uk
Web site   www.swishlife.co.uk

Mr Brian Richards
Owner/Buyer
Thackerays
251-255 Wellingborough Road
Northampton
NN1 4EH
01604 259889

Ms Deborah Campbell
Owner/Buyer
The Abbey
25 Abbeville Road
London SW4 9LA

The Bureau
46-50 Howard Street
Belfast
Northern Ireland BT1 6PG
+4402890326100
E-mail Address   sales@thebureaubelfast.com

Mr Steve Monaghan
Owner/Buyer
The Great Divide
Northgate House
2-8 Scrutton Street
London EC2A 4RT
0207 392 8860
E-mail Address   onfo@thegreat-divide.com
Web site   www.thegreat-divide.com

Ms Victoria Suffield
Owner/Buyer
The Hambledon
10 The Square
Winchester
Hampshire SO23 9ES
01962 890055
Web site   www.thehambledon.com

Mr Peter Sidell
Owner/Buyer
The Library
268 Brompton Road
Chelsea
London
0207 589 6569

Duffy .
The Menswear Buyer
The Three Threads
47 - 49 Charlotte Road
London EC2A 3QT
0207 749 0503
E-mail Address		info@thethreethreads.com
Web site		www.thethreethreads.com

The Menswear Buyer
Trapeze
50 Regent Street
Cheltenham GL50 1HA
01242 257325

Mr Gary Donaldson
The Menswear Buyer
Triads II
182 Linthorpe Road
Middlesbrough TS1 3RF
01642 254124

Mr Mats Klingberg
Managing Director
Trunk Clothiers
8 Chiltern Street
London W1U 7PU
0207 486 2357
Web site		www.trunkclothiers.com

The menswear Buyer
Unique
183 High Street
Bromley
Kent BR1 1NN
0208 313 1753

Mr Mark .
Owner/Buyer
Uno Ltd
30a High Street
Chislehurst
Kent BR7 5AN
0208 325 0807

Mr Mohammed Azam
Owner/Buyer
V2 Clothing
72 King William Street
Blackburn
Lancashire BB1 7DT
01254 264082

Mr Dean Walker
Menswear Buyer
Van Mildert
Unit 9-10 Easter Park
Barton Road Riverside Industrial Estate
Middlesborough TS2 1RY
0844 967 1028
E-mail Address   dean@vanmildert.com

Mr George Wade-Smith
Owner/Buyer
Wade - Smith
1st Floor The Hahnemann Building
42 Hope Street
Liverpool L1 9HW
0151 707 1220
E-mail Address   info@wade-smith.com
Web site   www.wade-smith.com

Mr Robert Wade-Smith
Owner/Buyer
Wade-Smith
1st Floor The Hahnemann Building
42 Hope Street
Liverpool L1 9HW
0151 707 1220
E-mail Address   info@wade-smith.com
Web site   www.wade-smith.com

Mr Tim Keating
Owner/Buyer
Weavers Door
1 Cavern Walks
Harrington Street
Liverpool L2 6RE
0151 236 6001
Web site   www.weaversdoor.com

Mr George Abayahoudayan
Owner/Buyer
Woodies
20 - 21 Duke Street
Brighton BN1 1AH
01273 776 777
E-mail Address   woodiesbrighton@yahoo.co.uk
Web site   www.woodiesbrighton.com

Mr Raymond Bacon
Owner/Buyer
Woodies Emporium
22 Morgan Arcade
Cardiff
South Glamorgan CF10 1AF
029 2023 2171

The Menswear Buyer
Woods of Chatham
Railway Street
Chatham
Kent ME4 4HU
01634 832147
E-mail Address sales@woodsdesignerclothing.com
Web site www.woodsdesignerclothing.com

Mr Jim Woodward
Owner/Buyer
Woodward Menswear
29 Station Road East
Oxted
Surrey RH8 0BD
01883 712733

Mr Richard Andrews
Owner/Buyer
Woosters
19 Mill Street
Oakham
Rutland LE15 6EA
01572 723697
E-mail Address   enquiries@woosters.co.uk
Web site   www.woosters.co.uk

Mr David Weeks
Owner/Buyer
Xile Clothing
42 Bridge Street
Edinburgh EH1 1LL
0131 225 6372
E-mail Address   mail@xileclothing.com
Web site   www.xileclothing.com

Mr Mel Pilkington
The Menswear Buyer
Y-3
54 Conduit Street
Mayfair
London W1S 2YY
0207 434 2324
E-mail Address customerservices@hervialondon.com
Web site   www.hervialondon.com

Mr Chris Geer
Owner/Buyer
Zagger Fashion Group
Baddow Road
Chelmsford
Essex CM2 0DG
01245 262 194
Web site   www.zagger.co.u

Mr Stuart Smith
Owner/Buyer
Zebra
17 Holywell Street
Chesterfield
Derbyshire S41 7SA
01246 271720
E-mail Address   zebramenswear@msn.com
Web site   www.zebramenswear.co.uk

The Menswear Buyer
Zee & Co Head Office
Unit 1
New Court Business Park, Perry Road
Harlow, Essex CM18 7NS
01279 432078
E-mail Address   estore@zeeandco.co.uk
Web site   www.zeeandco.co.uk

London Agents & Showrooms

Studio Thirteen
123 Ledbury Road
London W11 2AQ
0207 243 9395
Charlotte@studio-13.co.uk
www.studio-13.co.uk

Chiltern Street Studio
78b Chiltern Street
London W1U 5AB
0207 486 4800
Denise Tavernier
denise@chilternstreetstudio.com
www.chilternstreetstudio.com

Palladio Associates
Arch 210 Newnham Terrace
Hercules Road
London SE1 7DR
0207 633 9888
sales@palladioassociates.com
www.palladioassociates.com

Inexcess Fashion
Unit 4
124-128 Barlby Road
London W10 6BL
0208 960 6161
www.inexcessfashion.com

Emma Ellis Jones
20 Heathfield North
Twickenham
London TW2 7QW
07961 315969
info@ejellisjones.co.uk

Lucy Wernick Fashion Agency
11 Bowling Green Lane
Clerkenwell
London EC1 OBG
0207 580 8644
www.lwfa.co.uk

M&L Harris
10 -11 Greenland Place
London NW1 OAP
0207 428 3280
info@mlharris.co.uk
www.mlharris.co.uk

1927
1927 Building
2 Michael Road
London SW6 2AD
0207 384 1907
www.1927london.com
wendy@1927london.com

Rock it
3 Byewells Place
London
W1T 3DN
0207 636 6063

Area 142
29 Charlotte Road
London EC2A 3PF
0207 739 3573
debra@area142.com
www.area142.com

Claret Showroom
73 Uverdale Road
Chelsea
London
SW10 0SW
0207 349 8887
info@claretshowroom.co.uk
www.claretshowroom.co.uk

Rainbowwave
15 Flood Street
London SW3 5ST
0207 352 0002
www.rainbowwave.com
info@rainbowwave.com

Printed in Great Britain
by Amazon.co.uk, Ltd.,
Marston Gate.